TROUBLED WATERS

TROUBLED WATERS

The Real New Testament Theology of Baptism

Ben Witherington III

BAYLOR UNIVERSITY PRESS

© 2007 by Baylor University Press
Waco, Texas 76798

Cover Design by Jeremy Reiss

Library of Congress Cataloging-in-Publication Data

Witherington, Ben, 1951-
  Troubled waters : the real New Testament theology of baptism / Ben
Witherington.
    p. cm.
  Includes bibliographical references and index.
  ISBN 978-1-60258-004-6 (cloth/hardcover : alk. paper)
  1. Baptism--Biblical teaching. I. Title.

  BS2545.B36W58 2007
  234'.16109015--dc22
                                    2007009701

Printed in the United States of America on acid-free paper with a
minimum of 30% pcw recycled content.

CONTENTS

INTRODUCTION

I was working on my dissertation in Durham, England, and the phone rang. My wife and I were the caretakers of Elvet Methodist church, and we frequently received calls meant for the minister. The upper-class lady with the very proper British accent asked, "Do you do christenings?" My response was, "Of course, we do baptisms all the time." "No," she said, "nothing so elaborate as baptism. We just want a little water on the forehead of our wee one, you know." I tried to explain to her that christening, which is the shortened form of *christianing*, was a form of baptism, but she was not having it. She had this vision of immersing an infant. Needless to say, we had a problem of communication. The problem of baptism, particularly infant baptism, has always been an acute one in the church. Who should the recipients be, how much water should be used, and when should we undertake the rite?

I began my study of water baptism a very long time ago. In fact, I remember precisely when it began. I was doing my doctoral work at the University of Durham in England under C. K. Barrett. I needed a summer break from dealing with all those New Testament passages on women, but we were not going traveling this particular summer. So, on July 31, 1978, I decided to work through my questions and doubts as to the propriety of baptizing infants. I realized from the start that both the Baptist and Paedo-Baptist traditions have shipped a good deal of water over the centuries on this issue, if you will pardon a pun. The Paedo-Baptists, in practice if not in principle, have made the rite virtually synonymous with the Old Testament circumcision ritual or a dedicatory rite, while the Baptists have turned baptism into a Christian bar mitzvah. Working through all the elaborate arguments and issues bound up in understanding water baptism has taken a long time.

In such a situation, it seemed unlikely that the church would get very far in its discussion of the matter unless it recognized that no one has managed to avoid adapting the New Testament teaching on baptism without certain theological aberrations. The church needs reformation on this issue, as well as many others. The problem for Paedo-Baptists has been succinctly summed up with not a little humor by my former instructor, Dr. Roger Nicole: "In the New Testament we have some texts with infants but no baptism, and some texts with baptism but no infants." His comment puts a finger on a key point: the New Testament cannot "prove" infant baptism in the sense of producing clear examples of it from the text (unless "household baptism" implies this). The question then remains for the Paedo-Baptist whether or not the New Testament provides a pre-sacramental foundation for such a practice, so that infant baptism could be said to be a legitimate theological development from New Testament principles and practices that involve water baptism.

On the other hand, Baptists have a number of difficulties to face when confronted with the New Testament evidence. For instance, we have no examples in the New Testament showing the baptism of children of Christian parents at some time subsequent to the entrance of their parents into the church. Nor is there any discussion about an age of discretion or an age limit for the recipients of water baptism. Since the early church was primarily missionary in nature, there is no doubt that at first both Jew and Gentile entered the new covenant community from the outside. Another difficult question concerns to what degree the new covenant community is continuous or discontinuous with the old covenant community. This question is not answered by simply saying that the new covenant is "new," or by saying that the new covenant is simply the old one renewed under new management.

Unfortunately, the issue of water baptism has on the one hand been assumed to be a matter of little importance (see, for example, most Quakers or the Salvation Army), or on the other end of the spectrum a matter of ultimate importance with one's whole theology, particularly one's theology of salvation, hanging upon it (for example, Baptists and some high-church sacramentalists). The truth lies somewhere in between. Water baptism is a matter of importance for one's theology, but lest we overestimate its significance, we should remember the words of Paul to the Corinthians, "Is Christ divided? Was Paul crucified for you? Were you baptized into the name of Paul? I am thankful that I did not baptize any of you except Crispus and Gaius . . . for Christ did not send me to baptize but to preach the gospel . . ." (1 Cor 1:13-17, NIV).

Some of our squabbles over whether we should receive water baptism in Baptist or Paedo-Baptist fashion must appear to the Lord rather like the Corinthians dividing on the basis of who baptized them—regrettable to say the least. But the only way forward is not by ignoring our differences, but by sorting them out in light of the evidence of Scripture examined with an open heart and mind.

Some of the difficulties faced by all students of the New Testament teaching on water baptism should be mentioned from the start. First, we need to understand the relationship between water baptism and Spirit Baptism. In this matter James D. G. Dunn in his *Baptism in the Spirit* offers helpful suggestions. A related question is the problem of distinguishing when the New Testament is explicitly referring to water baptism and when texts are simply using baptismal language to speak of Spirit Baptism or some other aspect of Christian conversion or experience. We also need a clear understanding of the following issues: (1) What is the relationship between the Old Testament and the New Testament in principle and practice? (2) What is the New Testament view of the Christian family? (3) What is the New Testament view of the church and how one becomes a part of it? (4) Is water baptism an act of God, a response of a human being to the divine initiative, or both? These issues are addressed indirectly as the study requires, but they must always be kept in mind. Before beginning, I wish to thank those scholars who have devoted so much time and energy in the last thirty years to this issue.

This study is both indebted to and in reaction to the following important twentieth-century works on the subject. These works are referred to in the notes throughout this book:

1. The Barth-Cullmann debate: K. Barth, *The Teaching of the Church Regarding Baptism* (trans. E. A. Payne; London: SCM, 1948); O. Cullmann, *Baptism in the New Testament* (trans. J. K. S. Reid; London: SCM, 1950); K. Barth, *Church Dogmatics*, vol. 4, part 4 (trans. G. W. Bromiley; Edinburgh: T&T Clark, 1969).

2. The Jeremias-Aland debate: J. Jeremias, *Infant Baptism in the First Four Centuries* (trans. D. Cairns; London: SCM, 1960); K. Aland, *Did the Early Church Baptize Infants?* (trans. G. R. Beasley-Murray; London: SCM, 1963); J. Jeremias, *The Origins of Infant Baptism* (trans. D. M. Barton; London: SCM, 1963).

3. P. Marcel, *The Biblical Doctrine of Infant Baptism* (trans. P. E. Hughes; London: J. Clark, 1953).

4. G. R. Beasley-Murray, *Baptism in the New Testament* (Grand Rapids: Eerdmans, 1962).

5. P. K. Jewett, *Infant Baptism and the Covenant of Grace* (Grand Rapids: Eerdmans, 1978).

6. G. W. Bromiley, *Children of Promise—The Case for Baptizing Infants* (Grand Rapids: Eerdmans, 1979).

7. James Dunn, *Baptism in the Holy Spirit* (London: SCM, 1970).

Of course, other studies have been written before and since these, but these strike at the heart of the matter both exegetically and theologically and help provide us with answers to the sorts of practical questions that cause Baptist and Paedo-Baptist churches to stand on opposite sides of the baptismal waters in these matters. I am not interested in doing a definitive study of water baptism, only seeking to probe the core issues and see if some new insights and solutions can be offered to old dilemmas. As we shall see, this issue is mostly theological and historical, not exegetical, which is why I have chosen to focus on interacting primarily with historical and theological studies rather than with the commentaries. Too often the study of this issue only begins with early Jewish water rituals, and not with Old Testament theology itself. This study attempts to avoid that major mistake, so in some ways this is a study in biblical theology, not merely New Testament theology, although clearly the latter is the focus of our study.

One of my motivations for pursuing this matter is because now more than ever the church needs to get its act together and stop speaking with a forked tongue about crucial matters, lest the witness of our dividedness speak louder than the witness of what unites us to a fragmented and factious world that at least in the West is becoming rapidly less Christian. If we cannot even agree on the Christian entrance ritual—on the first steps and the rite of passage into the Christian community—then why should anyone listen to us on more central issues?

I approach this study with the realization that it will certainly not sort out all the knotty problems or convince all the audience one way or another. I hope at most to plant some seeds, hoping that with the proper "watering" they may grow down the road. It is time then to dive into our subject—head first. I trust the audience can swim!

—Christmas 2006

Chapter 1

GETTING OUR FEET WET

The Antecedents of Christian Baptism
outside the New Testament

FRANK ADMISSIONS AT THE POINT OF DEPARTURE

One surprise in studying the New Testament teaching on water baptism is the paucity of material dealing directly with the matter. Karl Barth points out, "With one significant exception, baptism is never a major theme."[1] The fact is, no New Testament document addresses itself to water baptism for its own sake. It is always mentioned as an illustration or exhortation to make some other point. One immediately thinks, "If baptism is all that important, why isn't there more discussion about its whys and wherefores, its mode and meaning?"

Often we find reference to water baptism or at least to the language of water baptism (being cleansed, being washed, putting on Christ, etc.) in ethical contexts. The reason that water baptism is always mentioned as a past fact rather than a present issue is that all the New Testament documents are addressed to people who already are baptized Christians. Other than a few brief exhortations in Acts, we have no addresses to pagans or Jews on this matter, and no documents addressed primarily or solely to proselytes. Accordingly we find virtually nothing in the New Testament to correspond to what we find in other early Christian documents such as the *Didache*. Here we read:

> Concerning baptism, baptize in the following manner: Having first rehearsed all these things, "baptize, in the Name of the Father and of the Son and of the Holy Spirit," in running water; but if you have no running water, baptize in other water, and if you can't in cold, then in warm. But if you have neither, pour water three times on the head "in the Name of the Father, Son, and Holy Spirit." And before the baptism let the baptizer and him who is to be baptized fast, and any others who are able. And you shall bid him who is to be baptized to fast one or two days before.[2]

Here is clear instruction to a community of Christians about how to baptize proselytes entering the community from without. But where do we find a clear statement of this kind in the New Testament telling us how, when, and who to baptize? To be sure there are hints on these matters in the language used and the theology presented of water baptism in the New Testament, and the passing references made. But the statements that we have in the New Testament on water baptism are primarily descriptive, not prescriptive, which is especially true of the often debated texts found in Acts. In Galatians, Colossians, Ephesians, 1 Peter, and 1 John, we have one or two references in each to water baptism, and these are not extensive. There is no mention of water baptism in 2 Corinthians, 1 or 2 Thessalonians, James, or Revelation. Even in the Pastoral Epistles—where we might expect to find such references when Paul addresses a future community leader (such as Timothy) on church practice—we find only one possible reference to water baptism in Titus 3:5, in a context of reflection on salvation history, not exhortation.

From what the gospels tell us, even Jesus did little more than to command that water baptism be an initiation rite of the new covenant community (Matt 28:19). Because water baptism is at most a secondary theme in the New Testament, used for illustration, ethical reinforce-ments, or theological development, we should realize that any deduc-tions about correct Christian practice of water baptism are drawn not from clear-cut prescriptive statements in the New Testament about how one ought to perform the rite, but from what one can conclude from various descriptive statements and *theologoumena* that reveal who was baptized then and what it meant.

This insight should be coupled with the fact that the New Testa-ment consists of missionary documents dealing with the beginnings of church history which by their nature do not address themselves to the problems of ensuing generations, when the church is a well-established entity with a well-defined order. Thus, any evaluation of the New Tes-tament evidence must proceed cautiously, recognizing that deducing a normative practice from primarily descriptive or purely theological statements is no easy task. Neither Baptists nor Paedo-Baptists can afford to overlook these facts.

This being so, we must first carefully examine possible antecedents to Christian baptism to see if they can fill in some necessary background before we examine the New Testament texts. I proceed in chronologi-cal order in this survey by looking at circumcision, proselyte baptism among Jews, the water rituals of the Qumran community, and finally the baptism of John. I have omitted the various initiation rites into pagan cults, especially the mystery cults, because I see no likelihood that the pagan mysteries are in the background of the Christian rite. They may, however, have influenced the development of language and thinking about baptism once Christianity began to have a significant Gentile element in its community.

CUTTING A COVENANT: CIRCUMCISION AS AN OLD TESTAMENT RITUAL AND CONTINUING JEWISH PRACTICE

Barth characterized circumcision in the following manner: "Circumci-sion refers to natural birth; it is the sign of the election of the holy lineage of Israel, which with the birth of the Messiah achieved its goal, so that therewith this sign lost its meaning."[3] Similarly, Beasley-Murray argues that circumcision "was administered to every male child in Israel as a sign of his membership in the covenant people and had no relation to moral renewal—the prophetic call for heart circumcision is an application of the rite in symbol, not an exposition of the rite itself."[4]

On the other side of the issue, P. Marcel argues adamantly:

> Circumcision was given to Abraham (and not to Moses) as a sign and seal of the justification which he obtained through faith by believing in the promises of the covenant of grace, and thus as a sign of the cleansing away of sins in the same way as is expressed by baptism today. . . . The significance of the rite of circumcision was thus spiritual also, not only because the sign was in harmony with the promise (of which it is precisely the sign and seal), but because of the spiritual meaning attributed to circumcision as representing at the same time the promise of God to circumcize the heart of the people and of their children. . . .[5]

Cullmann also avers: "[C]ircumcision is the seal of this faith of Abraham, thus from the outset envisaging the inclusion of the heathen world. . . . In fact circumcision is reception into the covenant . . . just as Christian baptism is reception into the Body of Christ."[6]

Between the first two authors and the last two, considerable difference arises as to what circumcision was and what it meant for the Jews. What then does the Old Testament have to say on the matter? The Old Testament evidence makes clear that circumcision is a sign of the covenant between God and Abraham and his descendants (Gen 17:11). Circumcision is a sign not only for those born within the household of Abraham and his natural descendants, but also for those "bought from a foreigner" (Gen 17:12).From the beginning, not only natural descendants, but also slaves or servants bought from non-Jews and brought into the household were to be included within the covenant community and to bear its sign. The principle is clear: "[A]ll your males must be circumcised" (Gen 17:10), whether born within the covenant community or entering from without. In this case only bought slaves are mentioned, but as time went on and foreigners joined the covenant community, they also received the sign—even when the Jews adopted the practice of proselyte baptism somewhere between the second century B.C. and the first century A.D. Circumcision was always a sign of the covenant for any born into or entering the "household of Abraham" and his descendants and thus cannot be fairly characterized as referring only to one's natural birth. If it was later understood as a badge of national pride or a sign of physical descent (denoting a sort of religious exclusiveness based on heredity), rather than a sign of the covenant, this interpretation is not because of something inherent in the nature of circumcision as a rite or sign. What was the significance of the sign that was to be "marked on your bodies as a covenant in perpetuity" (Gen 17:13)? G. Von Rad comments: "Human covenants also were accompanied by an external sign that obligated the parties to keep the agreement. . . . Thus . . . circumcision is only the act of appropriation, of witness to the revelation of God's salvation, and the sign of its acceptance."[7]

A great deal of light has been shed in the past fifty years on the significance of various aspects of Old Testament covenants through studies of ancient Near Eastern treaty documents drawn up by some of Israel's contemporaries. As many scholars have noted, there are striking parallels between the form of covenants in the Old Testament and of various Hittite Suzerainty treaties.[8] Meredith Kline, who has spent no little time studying the relation of those texts to covenants in the Old Testament, summarizes the significance of circumcision as revealed in Genesis 17 as follows:

> The practice of circumcision found earlier among other peoples was adopted to serve as the sign of incorporation into the Abrahamic covenant. Its continuing significance is learned from the function it performed at its institution. Covenants were ratified by oaths, the oath-curses being dramatized in symbolic rites (cf. 15:9 ff.). A

characteristic curse was that of cutting off the vassal to destruction and cutting off his name and seed. Accompanying this was a knife rite. So circumcision was the knife rite by which the Abrahamic covenant was cut. Gen. 17:14 shows that it symbolized the curse of excision from the covenant community. More precisely, the circumcision of the male organ of generation symbolized the cutting off of descendants. Yet as the sign of an oath acknowledging God's lordship, circumcision also signified consecration (cf. Rom. 4:11). Ancient vassal covenants included with the vassal king his kingdom and descendants. Similarly, the Lord administered his covenant to Abraham not simply as an individual believer-confessor but as the head of a community, in this case a family household, including children and slaves (vv. 12f., 23ff.), and that through ongoing generations (vv. 9, 12).[9]

Circumcision then is the sign of the ratification of a covenant which is not unilateral. God promises to Abraham to make him "the Father of a multitude of nations" (Gen 17:4, note the plural of "nations"). He promises "your issue shall be kings" (Gen 17:6). Most of all he vows to Abraham "to be your God and the God of your descendants after you. . . . I will give to you and to your descendants . . . the whole land of Canaan" (Gen 17:7-8). God commands Abraham to promise that "You on your part shall maintain my covenant yourself and your descendants" (Gen 17:9).

While the covenant is made with Abraham as an adult when he can respond in loyalty and faithfulness, its sign is to be applied to Abraham's male descendants on the eighth day after birth (Gen 17:12). Further, anyone within the covenant community but without the sign is to be "cut off from his people" (Gen 17:14), which likely means excommunication, not execution.[10] This sign was a reminder not only that the bearer of the sign was to give exclusive allegiance to Yahweh (whether he wanted to or not), nor merely that God promises its bearer the land of promise, but most importantly that Yahweh had sworn to be this person's God. To say then that the sign had "no relation to moral revival" or "spiritual" matters is not to do justice to this text. When God covenants and seals his covenant with the sign of circumcision, God calls his people to unswerving loyalty of the most moral nature. To "maintain the covenant" (Gen 17:9) involves a good deal more than a confession of faith. It involves a changed lifestyle consistent with the character of the God who initiated the covenant. Not surprisingly, elsewhere in the Old Testament the moral renewal that is implicit in Genesis 17 becomes explicit.

For instance, in Leviticus 26:41-42 we read, "I in my turn will set myself against them and take them to the land of their enemies. Then their uncircumcised heart will be humbled, then they will atone for their sins. I shall remember my covenant with . . . Abraham; and I shall remember the land." Note the element of being cut off from one's land and delivered into the hands of another people. Note that the uncircumcised heart refers to sins against God—a proud and stubborn rebellion against the mercies of God. Sin means that one fails to keep the covenant, rejecting the moral renewal to which the covenant calls him.

Note God's promise to remember the covenant and the land. There is a clear intermingling here of both the spiritual and the physical curses and blessings. It is unlikely that the writers of the Old Testament dichotomized (though they did at times distinguish) the physical and the spiritual when speaking either of the significance of the sign of the covenant, or of the blessing-and-curse sanctions involved when one obeys or violates the covenant. Most often, when the term *circumcised* was used to mean something more than the physical fact, it was used of humble submission to God's will and way, the first sign and act of which was submission to physical circumcision (cf. Deut 10:16, Jer 4:4, Ezek 44:7, where *uncircumcised in heart* means not just unchanged in attitudes, but also wicked in deeds). The reason the statements in the prophets about being uncircumcised in the heart had such force is not merely because of the scandal of rebellion against God, but also because the attitude and acts of the Jews contradicted what the sign of the covenant in their flesh signified, not merely a physical relation but also a promise to love and obey Yahweh, who loved and saved them. Note the force of Jeremiah's remarks in 9:24-26: "See, the days are coming—it is Yahweh who speaks—when I am going to punish all who are circumcised only in the flesh: Egypt, Judah, the Sons of Ammon, Moab, and all the Arabs who live in the desert. For all these nations, and the whole House of Israel too, are uncircumcised at heart."

G. Von Rad puts it this way: "The idea of circumcision as an act of bodily purification and dedication must also have played a role at times, otherwise the spiritualizing demand for a 'circumcision of the heart' could not have been made."[11] When Joshua circumcised the Israelites again after they entered the promised land (Josh 5:1ff.), he did so because none of those born in the wilderness had received the sign. It is said in Joshua 5:6 that the circumcised generation who came out of Egypt were not permitted to enter the promised land because "they had not obeyed the voice of Yahweh." Thus, they died in the wilderness. Part of that disobedience involved not circumcising their children, for "It was not the vicissitudes of the journey that caused the suspension of the rite of circumcision, but the gross disobedience of the generation which consequently perished in the wilderness."[12]

Once the next generation was circumcised by Joshua, Yahweh said to him, "Today I have taken the shame of Egypt away from You" (Josh 5:9). While the circumcised generation contradicted their sign's spiritual significance and demand and were thus "cut off from the land" of promise, the next generation received the sign as an indication of spiritual and physical blessing that takes away "the reproach of Egypt." This last phrase probably refers to the "reproach involved in the thoughts and sayings of the Egyptians that [God] had brought the Israelites out of Egypt to destroy them in the desert (Ex. 22.12; Num. 14.13-16; Deut. 9.28)."[13]

The sign of the covenant, a sign of cutting off, showed the Israelites that they were not cut off from their God and the spiritual and physical blessings that God conveyed, though their fathers had in fact been cut off in the desert. For this generation especially it was evident that circumcision was not just a sign of physical descent but a sign of the covenant and of spiritual and physical blessings that one had through a relationship with Yahweh. It was because of God's promises to Abraham, not merely the physical descent of the Israelites, that the covenant was renewed and relationship with God reestablished at Gilgal. The renewal was symbolized and ratified by circumcision. Once again, both the spiritual and the physical significance of the rite are underlined.

While circumcision was often thought of as a mark of distinction from the uncircumcised (1 Sam 14:6, 17:26, 36), to assume that this sign was intended to be merely a badge of natural birth or a sign of physical descent is mistaken. Israel was circumcised so that they could be a nation set apart for God and cut off from a godless world; distinguishing them from others was their special relationship to Yahweh and their special calling to believe in God and obey his commandments and proclaim that Yahweh alone was God. The blessing did not come from their special relationship to Abraham or some automatic benefit they derived from being his descendants.

Thus, while circumcision was certainly more of a sign of promise, baptism more a sign of fulfilled promise based on Jesus and his gift of the Spirit, trying to exalt baptism at the expense of circumcision is wrong, as is implying that faith, moral renewal, or God's fulfillment of His promises were totally absent in Old Testament times.[14] Paul himself was able to call Abraham's circumcision a sign or seal of faith. All the above must be kept in mind as our study of baptism progresses. A proper appreciation of New Testament ritual should not involve improper depreciation of an Old Testament ritual. This does not prejudge the issue of what elements of continuity or discontinuity exist between circumcision and baptism, but simply means we cannot a priori rule out elements of continuity between the two rites because they belong to different stages in God's dealings with humankind.

THE BRETHREN AND THE CISTERNS

The various water lustrations mentioned in the Old Testament, particularly in connection with sacrifices, likely provide us with some sort of background for the practice of proselyte baptism among the Jews and of the water lustrations of the Qumran community, if only in the way of a precedent for the use of water in an act of purification. Thus, we must briefly look at some of the relevant passages in the Old Testament.

When the Israelites were about to covenant with Yahweh at Mount Sinai, they were told to "prepare themselves today and tomorrow. Let them wash their clothing and hold themselves in readiness for the third day, because on the third day Yahweh will descend on the mountain of Sinai in the sight of all the people" (Exod 19:10-11). Even when this is done, however, the people are not allowed to go upon the mountain where Yahweh was (19:21). The priests also must purify themselves, but not even they are allowed to approach Yahweh on his holy mountain (19:22-24). Though Moses is told to bring Aaron with him when he comes up the mountain again (19:24), even Aaron is not allowed to approach Yahweh but with the elders must worship and look on God from a distance (24:1; cf. 24:9). Though Joshua does go up the mountain with Moses (24:13), it is only Moses God summons into his presence (24:16). Thus, whether the cleansing ritual actually prepared the Israelites to enter God's presence or simply prepared them for the whole covenanting act is not certain.

As Brevard Childs says, "They are to wash their clothes, an act which traditionally precedes a great and solemn happening (Gen 35:2; Josh: 3.5)."[15] There is no indication here that the water rite conveys holiness or in fact does anything more than prepare one physically for what follows in this instance. In Joshua 3:5 the water rite prepares one to be in the presence of God's holiness, and in Genesis 35:2 it is closely associated with a moral purification involving forsaking foreign gods and a moving to Bethel where the true God will be honored by an altar built in His name. Perhaps in this last passage we may see some background to the New Testament teaching or language of baptism, for Jacob's family is told to "wash and change your clothes," reminding one of the New Testament language—especially of Paul who speaks of "putting on Christ" or being "clothed with Christ," no doubt drawing on such language. In Genesis 35:2, we have an outward and physical act of washing and changing clothes connected with a spiritual and physical act of giving up of foreign gods and proceeding to Bethel to build an altar to Yahweh.

Of a somewhat different nature are the instructions given to Moses for Aaron in Leviticus 16:3-4: "This is how he is to enter the sanctuary. . . . He is to put on a tunic of consecrated linen . . . and a linen turban on his head. These are the sacred vestments, he must put on after washing himself with water." This is the procedure for the Day of Atonement and it must be followed, for "Aaron . . . must not enter the sanctuary beyond the veil . . . whenever he chooses. He may die; for I appear in a cloud on the throne of mercy" (16:2). Further, when Aaron has completed the act of atonement, he must leave his consecrated clothes in the sanctuary and wash his body in a consecrated place (16:24).

Verses 3-4 contain a sense of ritual purification that apparently also involves moral purification, whether through or with the washing. But in verse 24 we apparently have the concept of God's presence conveying holiness to Aaron and his consecrated clothes, a holiness that must remain in the sanctuary lest it come into contact with unholy people outside and affect them in some drastic way.[16] This concept is perhaps confirmed when we observe the very similar thought in Ezekiel 44:15-19: "[W]hen they go out to the people in the outer court they are to remove the vestments in which they have performed the liturgy and leave them in the rooms of the Holy Place and put on other clothes, so as not to hallow the people with their vestments" (v. 19).

The regulations in regard to purifying ordinary people center, as Beasley-Murray has rightly noted, on the processes of birth (including intercourse), sickness, and death.[17] These rules were originally limited to cleansing after intercourse (Lev 15:8), or menstruation (Lev 15:12), or coming into contact with anyone who is sick with certain diseases (Lev 13, leprosy) or the dead (Num 5:1; 19:1; 31:19). Such rules were later expanded in great detail by the rabbis, as even a cursory examination of the sixth division of the Mishnah (Tohoroth) will reveal. The point of the Law of Holiness in Leviticus 17–26 is not simply that Yahweh demanded ritual purity of his priests or people in general. Ritual purifying regulations are interspersed with laws about moral and spiritual purity (19:1; 20:26-27; 24:10), or purity that affected one's economic policies (25:33ff.). The point of all such regulations is made clear by the constant refrain, "be holy for I Yahweh your God am holy" (Lev 19:2), or "be consecrated to me because I Yahweh am holy, and I will set you apart from all these peoples so that you may be mine" (Lev 20:26). Yahweh's people are in every facet of their being to be like Yahweh—holy, set apart, clean, pure. It is surely right then to say of these regulations: "The intention of the book was not to secure ritual purity alone nor obedience as a bare religious principle, still less ethical purity divorced from the other two, but to serve all three together."[18]

In the Old Testament, then, the language of bodily purification by water can be used to refer to inward moral or spiritual purification, as in the beautiful Psalm 51:6ff. Similarly, such language can be used in an oracle that speaks of a final and complete gathering of God's people and cleansing of them "body, soul, and spirit": "I shall pour clean water over you and you will be cleansed; I shall cleanse you of all your defilement and all your idols. I shall give you a new heart, and put a new spirit in you" (Ezek 36:25-26). In both of these instances it is doubtful that a literal washing of the body is in view at all. Rather, the language of cleansing by water is used to describe a more significant cleansing, or as we have noted before, the outward cleansing only has meaning through its association with the spiritual or moral cleansing it symbolizes.[19]

It is surely no accident that when we get to New Testament times, we find evidence of mikvehs everywhere—at Qumran, on Masada, outside the walls of Jerusalem—in fact, in most any place where ritual cleansing was needed before a religious act was going to be undertaken. The ritual purity was seen as precursor to and sign of the spiritual purity that only God could effect. Early Jews clearly felt the presence of enough impurity in the land and in themselves that they needed regular cleansing. This situation is understandable when one is an occupied people, and all the more so when one sees one's people plagued not only literally by unclean rulers, but also spiritually by unclean spirits. Into this environment John the Baptizer and Jesus came.

CROSSING JORDAN: JEWISH PROSELYTE BAPTISM

One of the most controversial subjects that relates to the discussion of Christian water baptism is the matter of Jewish proselyte baptism. Particularly, the question of when this practice originated is hotly debated. Even the advocates of an early date for its inception admit that the first clear reference to the practice originates in the first century A.D.[20] On the other hand, by far the majority of scholars believe that this practice is pre-Christian in origin, as Beasley-Murray openly admits.[21] The chief argument against seeing a pre-Christian origin for this rite is from silence—the silence of Philo, Josephus, and perhaps also the New Testament (but cf. below on Heb 6:1-6).

Certain factors in the New Testament, however, may lend us indirect evidence on this subject. The uncleanness of the Gentiles was taken for granted among Jews in New Testament times (cf. John 18:28; Acts 10:28, 11:12, and perhaps Matt 8:7-8). Of what sort this uncleanness was is not completely clear, though it appears that a Gentile was not considered Levitically unclean since he was not under Levitical law. Thus, while proselyte baptism might not relate to a washing away of Levitical uncleanness, seeing it as a rather supplementary initiation or purification rite is wrong. In his classic study, G. F. Moore writes: "The rite has a superficial analogy to the many baths prescribed in the law for purification after one kind or another of religious uncleanness."[22] Moore also remarks of the proselyte: "As soon as he was circumcised and baptized he was in full standing in the religious community . . . He had entered into the covenant."[23]

The truth of this statement, at least in some Jewish circles in the first century A.D., is perhaps illustrated in the following saying from the Talmud: "If he assents to all, they circumcise him at once, and when he is healed, they baptize him, and two scholars stand by, and tell him of some of the light and of some of the heavy laws. When he has been baptised, he is regarded in all respects as an Israelite" (*b. Yebam.* 47b). This quote reflects one of the discussions between the schools of Shanmiai and Hillel (both of whose founders lived in the decades of the first century B.C.), for it subscribes to the Hillelite practice of separating baptism from circumcision by an interval of a week, making baptism the climactic act in joining the Jewish community.[24] If it is true that the impurity the Hillelites assigned to Gentiles was the impurity of a corpse, then it would appear that water baptism may have had the significance of cleansing away the dead man and his defilement (cf. *m. 'Ohal.* 18.7; *Pesah* 8.8; *'Ed.* 5.2). Further, we know through Talmudic quotations of the familiar rabbinic phrase, that "[t]he proselyte in his conversion is like a newborn child" (*b. Yebam.* 48b; *Sifre* 91a).[25] The proselyte and any children born after the proselyte's baptism are said to be in a state of holiness. Besides these points, other detailed theological correspondences occur between what is said of proselyte baptism by the rabbis and what is said of Christian baptism in the New Testament, as Jeremias has shown.[26]

Though the practice of proselyte baptism in the first half of the first century A.D. or the influence on Christian baptism of the theology and catechesis of conversion used by the Jews is not disputed by Beasley-Murray,[27] he does dispute that it was as widespread or had the effect on who Christians would baptize that Jeremias tried to demonstrate. I am willing to say that during the first Christian century proselyte baptism became an important if not the decisive mark of conversion for a proselyte, perhaps due to the increasing influence of the Hillelites.

Most if not all of the documents in the New Testament were written subsequent to A.D. 50, and people such as Paul, the author of

Hebrews, or Jewish Christians in Acts, for instance, might indeed be quite influenced in their principles and practices of baptism by Jewish proselyte baptism. While proselyte baptism may not have influenced the origins of Christian baptism, it may well have affected its development. True enough, Christian baptism had a special significance because of its association with the death of Jesus and union with Christ made possible through the Spirit, but even these distinctions of Christian theology have points of contact with Jewish theology of conversion, initiation, and perhaps proselyte baptism.[28] Thus, simply because of some theological differences in what water baptism signified in the cases of Jewish and Christian practice, respectively, this does not by any means rule out the possibility that Christianity owed not only the mode of its baptism, but also its possible recipients, to Jewish proselyte baptism practices (another fact that Beasley-Murray does not dispute).

The practice of late rabbinic Judaism was to baptize the infants of proselytes with their parents as they entered the covenant community. No direct mention of this practice appears prior to A.D. 250. There is no dispute, however, that male Gentile infants of proselytes were circumcised with their parents as they entered the covenant community in even pre-Christian times.[29] Though we cannot be certain if the Hillelite view prescribed that a proselyte must have both circumcision and baptism on entrance to the community, with baptism becoming the climactic mark of becoming part of the covenant for them, it seems quite probable that at least in some cases in New Testament times infants of Jewish proselytes were being baptized. This conclusion is reasonably deduced from the fact that circumcision and baptism were both part of Jewish initiation procedure and that no more than seven days separated these two rites, one of which was certainly applied to all male proselytes and their children at this time. In view of numerous correspondences between Jewish proselyte and Christian baptism in mode, catechetical teaching, and some of its theological significance, we conclude that there may well have been a precedent for water baptism in New Testament times in the practice of Jewish proselyte baptism. Whether or not Christians adopted this precedent is something we cannot rule out on the basis of the evidence thus far examined. That discussion must wait for our examination of the New Testament evidence.

LUSTRATIONS BY THE DEAD SEA: THE QUMRAN COMMUNITY

In New Testament scholarship some fifty years ago, drawing parallels between the Qumran community and the Christian community of New Testament times was thought to be the quickest way to understand rightly certain principles and practices of the New Testament. The parallels between Qumran and Christian practices, however, in the matter of water rites have never been considered a major point of contact between the two groups. For one thing, the water lustrations of Qumran took place not simply once in a lifetime or even once in a day, but as many as three times a day if we are to believe Josephus.[30] This practice was perhaps in place because of the priestly origins of this sect of Judaism.[31]

Apparently, the primary function of most if not all of these lustrations was to remove ceremonial uncleanness caused by contact with unclean people or objects. In the Damascus rule we are told, "No man entering the house of worship shall come unclean and in need of washing" (*Damascus Document* 11). After the last apocalyptic battle, the Sons of light will "wash their garments and shall cleanse themselves of the blood of the bodies of the ungodly" (*War Scroll* 14).

A purification rite was also connected with entrance into the community of Qumran. Geza Vermes writes, "This seems to have been a peculiar and solemn act similar to Christian baptism, and to have symbolized purification by the 'spirit of holiness.'"[32] Several features about this rite are important. The person who sought entrance into the community had to "undertake by a binding oath to return with all his heart and soul to every commandment of the Law of Moses" (*Community Rule* V). This act was done without compulsion, for the Qumran community always described themselves as having freely pledged this allegiance to God and the Mosaic Law as interpreted by the "Sons of Zadok." This pledge of allegiance involved the proselyte in a renunciation, "And he shall undertake by the Covenant to separate from all men of falsehood who walk in the way of wickedness" (*Community Rule* V). If a proselyte swears to do these things he shall, "enter the water to partake of the pure Meal of the saints"(*Community Rule* V). Vermes writes, "it may be deduced that this baptism was to take place in 'seas and rivers' . . . like the baptism of John and Jesus, and that true conversion was the absolute condition for the efficacy of the sacrament."[33] The Qumran community did not believe that new water purified a person if he was wicked, nor were they striving only after outward purity. As *Community Rule* III says:

> for whoever ploughs the mud of wickedness returns defiled. He shall not be justified by that which his stubborn heart declares lawful, for seeking the ways of light he looks towards darkness. He shall not be reckoned among the perfect; he shall neither be purified by atonement, nor cleansed by purifying waters, nor sanctified by seas and rivers, nor washed clean with any ablution. Unclean, unclean shall he be. For as long as he despises the precepts of God he shall receive no instruction in the Community of His counsel.

The parallels of some of these ideas to New Testament material are notable (Eph 5:26; Heb 10:22; 1 Pet 3:21, etc.).

Our comments on these parallels must be reserved for our discussion of the New Testament material itself. Beasley-Murray speaks of the Qumranites in this fashion: "It is remarkable to what extent the sectaries succeeded in maintaining this conjoint emphasis on ritual cleansing and moral endeavour."[34] Perhaps he would have found it a little less remarkable if he had not occasionally caricatured Old Testament and early Jewish religion as a religion that did not connect or relate ritual and moral purity. This first cleansing of the Qumran initiate was more than just a first bath; it was the entrance into the "purity of holy men" if the proper moral rectitude accompanied the act. In this particular water rite, then, we do find a point of contact with the practice of John the Baptizer, and to him and his water rite we must now turn.

Chapter 2

JOHN'S BAPTISM—
TOTALLY IMMERSED IN HIS WORK

Pre-Christian Initiations in the New Testament and Pre-sacramental Texts

JOHN, JOHN QUMRAN'S SON

And so John came, baptizing in the desert region and preaching repentance and baptism for the forgiveness of sins. The whole Judean countryside and all the people of Jerusalem went out to him. Confessing their sins, they were baptized by him in the Jordan. . . . And this was his message: "After me will come one more powerful than I, the thongs of whose sandals I am not worthy to stoop down and untie. I baptize you with water, but he will baptize you with the Holy Spirit." (Mark 1:4-5, 7-8, NIV)

Perhaps it was his camel-hair garment or his diet of locust and wild honey (Mark 1:7), or the way he denounced the Pharisees and Sadducees as a "brood of vipers" (Matt 3:7), or even his clarion call "repent for the Kingdom of heaven is near" (Matt 3:1), that has given the impression that John the Baptizer was primarily a prophet of apocalyptic doom. But in fact, John's word was a two-edged sword, for the coming of the kingdom meant not only judgment and redemption, but also a redemptive-judgment that purified those it saved as well as scorching those it condemned (Matt 3:12). This is perhaps why in Matthew 3:11 John says that the Coming One will baptize not only with Spirit but also with fire, the latter being a clear symbol of judgment.

What led John to preach the nearness of the kingdom, to call even "good" Jews to repentance and baptism in preparation for this kingdom? Of all the possible influences in Judaism at this time that could have led to such a ministry, the principles and practices of the Qumran community seem the most likely wellspring from which John arose. As Beasley-Murray says:

> There is a bridge from Qumran to John the Baptizer and it has more than one track: for the Covenanters and for John, the End is near; it requires drastic moral preparation; and lustration apart from the Temple worship, albeit necessarily conjoined with repentance, is effective for that purpose. In each case John is more radical in his teaching and more genuinely prophetic; but the Covenanters prepared the Way of the Lord better than they knew—by preparing the way of the Forerunner.[1]

If for no other reason than the fact that Jesus underwent the baptism of John, we should study the origins and meaning of John's practice. In the Lukan narrative we are told that John was born in the Judean hill country and brought up in the wilderness (Luke 1:5-80). In fact, Luke writes that John lived in the desert until he appeared publicly to Israel (1:80). When we next hear of John, he is not following in his father's footsteps, exercising priestly office in the Temple, but living a semi-ascetical and nomadic existence, preaching and administering a baptism for repentance.[2] The question that must be raised is: How is it that John became an ascetical prophet instead of an establishment priest? The most probable answer is that John, like a considerable number of others who were members of priestly families, "was sent (on the death, perhaps, of his parents?) to be reared in the desert discipline of the Qumran Community."[3]

All four gospels associate the words of Isaiah 40:3 with John: "A voice cries in the wilderness: prepare a way for the Lord, make his paths straight" (Matt 3:3; Mark 1:3; Luke 3:4; John 1:23). In fact, in the Johannine account, John the Baptizer characterizes himself in the terms of this phrase. Strikingly, the Qumran community also used this very same Old Testament verse to describe and justify their aims (Manual of Discipline 8:14; 9:9). Particularly in the Manual of Discipline, the use of this verse has an eschatological form to it. The point of the Qumran Community was to go out into the wilderness "to prepare the way of Yahweh in the desert, to announce the imminent coming of the Prophet, and to gather the faithful of Israel for a final dedication to their God."[4] The Qumran community, like John, foresaw a near eschaton that would involve judgment on Israel unless they repented. Accordingly, both directed their ministry not to Gentile proselytes but to Jews. The concept of a prepared righteous few comes to the surface in the ministry and practices of both Qumran and John.

While no single baptism was used for the removal of sins in Qumran, we have seen that the initial washing of the initiate did have the character of renouncing the ways of the world (repentance) and an entry into the covenant and into the purity of the holy ones. On the basis of John 3:25 one may wish to ask whether in fact John's rite was seen as a once and once only ritual, or simply another one of the water lustrations about which his disciples are talking.

John, as at Qumran, had a strong stress on the need for prior repentance, as is seen in some of the quotes mentioned at the beginning of this chapter, and for both John and the Qumranites the true purified and prepared Israel was not built simply on racial inheritance, but on a gathered and repentant group of those loyal to Yahweh (Matt 3:9; Luke 3:8). Also, like the Qumranites, John saw the initial washing of the repentant one as a preparation for a greater baptism or cleansing. This future and eschatological baptism was to be administered by one coming after him who would baptize with the Holy Spirit (Mark 1:8; John 1:33) or the Holy Spirit and fire (Matt 3:11; Luke 3:16). So said John. but this claim is also intimated in the Qumran literature, as we have already noted. Compare now the translation of the *Manual of Discipline* by T. Gaster: "Then too, God will purge all the acts of man in the crucible of His truth; and refine for Himself all the fabric of man, destroying every spirit of perversity from within his flesh and cleansing him by the Holy Spirit from all the effects of wickedness. Like waters of purification he will sprinkle upon him the Spirit of truth."[5]

In this one quote we have a microcosm of the Baptizer's preaching involving cleansing, water, and the Holy Spirit in the context of judgment, fire, and the purifying of all wickedness. Jesus described John's baptism or his ministry and teaching as "the way of righteousness" (Matt 21:32; cf. Luke 7:29ff.), and this phrase may have been "more technical than has hitherto been suspected."[6] In fact, it may have derived from such Qumran sayings about the function of the spirit of truth in a person, as "that all the paths of true righteousness may be made straight before him, and that fear of the laws of God may be instilled in his heart" (*Manual of Discipline* 8:14, cf. 9:9). It is even possible that John derived his belief in a "Coming One" who would be a suffering servant (see John 1:29) and who would be anointed with the Holy Spirit (John 1:32ff.) from the Qumran community belief that they were a community set apart to embody the servant ideal and make atonement for earth and to be anointed with the Holy Spirit. There may even have been a belief among the Qumranites that this ideal could be embodied in one eschatological figure (cf. *Community Rule* IV:20-23 to IV:2 and VIII:4-8).

Without underestimating all these probable and possible parallels, John the Baptizer was very much a unique figure as well. If he was a part of the Qumran community, then he did not stay with them. He did not permanently withdraw into the desert to get away from the impurity of Israel, but to call Israel to a purification against the imminent coming of the kingdom. Further, John's stress on the Coming One baptizing with Spirit has no parallel in Qumran. There is also some evidence that John, like Jesus, associated with tax collectors, harlots, and other sinners to bring them to repentance (cf. Matt 21:31-32). Nonetheless, there is a strong element of Qumran in John's ministry and message, and thus this Qumran evidence serves to confirm the gospel's description of him in many ways.[7]

How then are we to assess John's water baptism and his prophecy of Spirit Baptism? In the first place, the gospels are clear that John's baptism is preparatory. It does not usher one into the kingdom; it only prepares one to enter when it comes. This distinction is made clear especially in the contrast found in the gospels between John's water baptism and the Coming One's Spirit Baptism. "I baptize with water, but (*de*) he will baptize in Holy Spirit" (Mark 1:8; Matt 3:11; Luke 3:16). This is confirmed by such statements as Matthew 3:1: "Repent for the Kingdom of heaven is near."[8] A second key point is that John's baptism was "not a repentance baptism which results in the forgiveness of sins, but John's baptism is the expression of the repentance which results in the forgiveness of sins."[9] John, like the Qumranites, recognized that water baptism did not produce forgiveness of sins. Indeed, Josephus described it as a baptism used not "to gain pardon for whatever sins they committed, but as a consecration of the body implying that the soul was already thoroughly cleansed by right behavior" (*Ant.* 18.5.2).

While this may be going a bit too far, clearly neither John nor those he baptized thought that the act of baptism conveyed forgiveness. Rather, it conveyed repentance and appealed for forgiveness.[10] Further, John's baptism is never connected with Christian water baptism in the gospels; rather it foreshadows and depicts the baptism in Spirit and fire that Jesus was to bring. Mark 1:8 and its parallels are enough to show that *baptidzein* need not necessarily refer to water baptism, which is crucial to bear in mind when we later discuss a number of passages in the gospels and Paul.

John's baptism was a rite "which served as a vivid and expressive figure of the coming judgement."[11] It pointed to the coming outpouring of the Spirit for redemption and judgment. In seeing the water rite as a figure of judgment, John and the gospel writers may have been drawing on the Old Testament and ancient Near Eastern concept of trial by water ordeal. As we shall see when we discuss 1 Peter 3:21,

Noah's salvation experience could be called a trial by water ordeal, or a redemptive-judgment in which the flood waters served to judge some but save others (as we remarked earlier on Matt 3:12 and the Spirit's coming). Israel's experience in the Red Sea, while it involves the salvation of Israel, also involves the judgment of Egypt (cf. 1 Cor 10:1ff.). Both of these water ordeals are seen as types of Christian baptism in the New Testament. Frequently in the Old Testament language, immersion or drowning is used to describe the judgment of God (cf. Ps 42:7; Jonah 2:3, etc.). Thus, perhaps John's baptism was seen as a symbol of God's redemptive-judgment looking back on Old Testament water ordeals, and forward to baptism in Spirit and fire. Just as in the old covenant, one applied the visible symbol of the oath curse of cutting off (circumcision) as a means of consecrating and dedicating oneself to God, so here John's baptism may have conjured up images of a divine redemptive-judgment as well as an opportunity for consecration.

In a sense, then, John's baptism may be seen as a "recircumcision" in preparation for the wrath and Spirit to come. In any case, Dunn is surely right when he says of John's baptism:

> It does not mark the beginning of the eschatological event; it does not initiate into the new age; it is the answer to John's call for preparedness; by receiving the Preparer's baptism the penitent prepares himself to receive the Coming One's baptism. It is the latter alone which initiates the Kingdom and initiates into the Kingdom. The baptism in Spirit-and-fire is the tribulation through which all must pass before the Kingdom can be established and before the penitent can share in the blessings of the Kingdom.[12]

Because of the clear contrasts in the gospel between John as forerunner and Jesus as the Coming One (cf. Luke 16:10 and Matt 11:1-13; note the "until" in both passages); between John's water baptism and Jesus' Spirit and fire baptism; between the one who testifies not of himself, and the one who is called the Lamb of God; between the kingdom drawing near, and the kingdom being in Jesus' person, it is quite wrong to assert, as Beasley-Murray does, that John's baptism inaugurates the eschatological event.[13] Only Spirit Baptism can do that. One can argue that the presentation of John in these gospels is slanted in Jesus' favor, but even if this is so, we have to say then that the earliest Christian interpretations of John's baptism do not match up with Beasley-Murray's.

Even less can we say with K. Barth, "Those baptised by John in the Jordan were as such truly saved, invited and summoned to faith in Jesus Christ. Accepting John's baptism, they made in fact a genuine confession of Jesus Christ."[14] Nor is it at all likely, as Barth contends, that Jesus himself is baptized into his own name when he submitted to John's baptism.[15] Rather, we must follow the more sober statement made by Barth that those baptized by John were making "their factual declaration that they await and need thorough cleansing."[16]

If one were to look for the most likely antecedent for Christian baptism, it is undoubtedly John's baptism, for several reasons. First, the Fourth Evangelist tells us that two of Jesus' disciples came from among the disciples of John—Andrew and one other (the beloved disciple? John 1:35-40). Second, the Fourth Evangelist also speaks of a separate and competing baptism to John's—that of the disciples of Jesus who were likely adopting John's practice (cf. John 3:22-26; 4:1-3). If the dispute mentioned in John 3:25 is about the relative merits of John's and Jesus' (or that of his disciples') baptism, then the two are closely related at least in the disputer's mind (and perhaps the evangelist's), for they both fall under the label of "ceremonial washing."

The phrase *ceremonial washing* indicates that both were thought of as falling within the category of the Jewish system of purifications, which would be only natural.[17] In any event, when Jesus gave the command, "Go and make disciples of all nations, baptizing . . ." (Matt 28:19), more than likely the disciples understood that they should continue the practice they had undergone with John or learned from John or did in parallel to what John's disciples were doing. This is confirmed perhaps in the language first used with Christian baptism in Acts, for it is very reminiscent of the words of John: "Repent and be baptized every one of you . . . so that your sins may be forgiven. And you will receive the Holy Spirit" (cf. Acts 2:38 to Matt 3:2, 11; Mark 1:4, 8; Luke 3:3). Perhaps the most important reason that John's baptism should be seen as the original antecedent of Christian baptism is because Jesus himself underwent it. But this raises some pointed questions about what such an act could have meant to Jesus himself.

There are three questions one must ask about John's baptism of Jesus: (1) Why did Jesus submit to it? (2) What was its significance for him? (3) What was its relation to the anointing of the Spirit that Jesus experienced immediately after having received the water baptism? As we begin to think about the first question, bear in mind that Jesus was an adult when he received John's baptism, and he likely would have heard of what John was doing at the Jordan and what he was saying long before he actually approached John to be baptized. Luke tells us that Jesus and John were closely related. This makes Jesus' detailed knowledge of him beforehand all the more likely (see Luke 1:5-80). This relationship also explains why all the gospels reveal that John knew not only who Jesus was when he came for baptism, but also what he was meant to be. In short, Jesus' going to the Jordan was not likely a spur-of-the-moment decision.

Further, Jesus was knowledgeable in Scriptures from an early age (Luke 2:41-52), and it seems likely that Jesus knew that John's preaching of a near kingdom meant not only redemption but also judgment for Israel and that John's baptismal rite prepared for this (perhaps drawing on the familiar associations of immersion with God's judgment). If Luke 2:41-52 is at all an accurate portrayal of Jesus' youth, then Jesus early on had a sense that he was to have a special role in God's plan of salvation history. Perhaps when Jesus heard of John's preaching of a Coming One who would baptize with Holy Spirit and fire, he recognized that he was being called to ministry. All this is conjectural, but not improbable.

In only one of the gospel accounts are we told why Jesus submitted to John's baptism. In the words of Jesus himself, "Let it be so now; it is proper for us to do this to fulfill all righteousness" (Matt

3:15). It is most unlikely that either the baptismal scene or these words would have been invented by the evangelist, because of the difficulties that were later recognized of a sinless Messiah receiving the baptism of repentance for the forgiveness of sins. What did Jesus mean by his statement? In the first place, the phrase *it is proper or fitting* probably refers to the fact that Jesus saw this act as fulfilling or submitting to God's will. Most commentators rightly note that this was Jesus' way of expressing his solidarity with sinners in their plight.[18] But it was also more than that; it was a baptism in preparation for the coming kingdom, the coming divine judgment, a way for its participants to submit to the righteousness of God's judgment upon them, to express a hope for God's mercy. If Jesus only saw his water baptism as a vow to lead the righteous life thereafter, or as a religious duty, then this "in no way explains how he related it to his vocation."[19]

Perhaps John the Baptizer himself explains what this act symbolized when he said, "Behold the Lamb of God who takes away the sin of the world" (John 1:29). Perhaps John was referring to the Old Testament idea of the lamb as a leader of the flock. The taking away of sin need not refer to the rejection of Messiah or his sacrificial death.[20] But considering that John was the son of a priest, that he may have associated with a community of those who had priestly connections (Qumran), and that the concept of a sacrificial lamb was well known in Judaism (cf. Exod 12:5, 29:39; 2 Sam 12:3; Isa 53:7; Jer 11:19), and especially in light of the Abraham and Isaac story (Gen 22:1ff.), it seems improbable that John would have had no thought of a sacrifice, even an atoning sacrifice, when he referred to Jesus in these words at his baptism.[21]

Perhaps then Jesus did see his baptism as the first step on the way of the cross. If John's words are even close to historically accurate and Jesus accepted a baptism that identified him with sinners and depicted in part the judgment or oath curse on those sinners, then it seems likely that Jesus meant by "fulfilling all righteousness" being obedient to God's righteous will, which in due course would even mean "obedient unto a death on the cross" (Phil 2:8). Perhaps, humanly speaking,

Jesus only began to see the necessity of death to fulfill the claims of God's righteousness at this point, and by accepting this baptism was expressing a willingness to do whatever was fitting, whatever was God's will for him as he identified with sinners. This act prepared him for his ministry to sinners. If one looks at Mark 10:38 (cf. Luke 12:50) where Jesus speaks of death, his death, as a baptism, this suggests that he did indeed see baptism as an image of death.

An act that was to follow, an act of the Father, indeed equipped Jesus for that ministry. It is perhaps the great fault of many interpretations of Jesus' water baptism that it is too readily confused with anointing of the Spirit that followed. The gospel writers are in fact very careful to distinguish between the two, though not to dichotomize them, for they were both part of one process. For instance, Matthew 3:16 describes Jesus' Spirit anointing in this way: "As soon as Jesus was baptized he went up out of the water. At that moment heaven was opened and he saw the Spirit of God descending." Mark 1:10 puts it this way: "As Jesus was coming up out of the water, he saw heaven torn open and the Spirit descend." Once again it is after the act of water baptism, when Jesus is leaving the water behind, that this second event takes place. Luke 3:21-22 reveals that the coming of the Spirit happened after Jesus was baptized and while he was praying. It seems unlikely that he prayed during immersion (John does not refer to immersion, but the parallels make this connection likely). Finally, John gives the clearest testimony to the distinction between the two acts by mentioning only the descent of the Spirit directly (1:32).

To use Dunn's words, "In short, a decisive 'shift in the aeons' has taken place . . . at Jordan when Jesus was anointed with the Spirit. It is after this event that the note of fulfilment enters: Jesus' first words in Mark's gospel are, "The time . . . is fulfilled . . .' (1.15). . . .'"[22] As to the eschatological feature, Dunn says, "The rending of the heavens, a common feature of apocalyptic writing, indicates a breaking through from the heavenly realm to the earthly."[23]

Note that this did not take place before or during the act of immersion, for these were events that preceded the eschatological breaking in. Also remember that the voice from heaven spoke not while Jesus was receiving water baptism, but after the Spirit descended on Jesus. Everything about the Spirit anointing links the event to the breaking in of the eschatological age. Besides the voice from heaven, the descending dove quite possibly is meant to remind us of the dove sent out by Noah after the water ordeal he faced. As such, it symbolized a new beginning, a new creation, or as Dunn says, "even a new covenant—in the eschatological circumstances, the new covenant."[24]

Furthermore, there is the heavenly voice, "You are my beloved son in whom I am well pleased." (Mark 1:11; Luke 3:22, note that Matt 3:17 has, "This is my son"). It is likely wrong to see in this quote only an allusion to Isaiah 42:1 instead of a combined allusion to Psalm 2:7 and Isaiah 42:1. If this is a combined allusion, then in some sense at this point Jesus assumes the mantle of the Christ (the Anointed One), though not in some adoptionist sense. In fact, however, at the Jordan Jesus begins to take on the role of Messiah. Dunn urges:

> The descent of the Spirit on Jesus effects not so much a change in Jesus, his person or his status, as the beginning of a new stage in salvation-history. The thought is not so much of Jesus becoming what he was not before, but of Jesus entering where he was not before—a new epoch in God's plan of redemption—and thus, by virtue of his unique personality, assuming a role which was not his before because it could not be his by reason of the kairos being yet unfulfilled.[25]

The idea of the Servant theme of Isaiah 42:1 is not wholly absent from this scene. Jesus is clearly depicted as messiah here and uniquely the Son of God, but the way he was to express these facts was as the Servant—a representative of the people who had already identified himself with their sins. Thus, the Spirit-anointed Jesus is empowered to teach, to heal, to endure temptation and death, not merely to meet the demands of all righteousness but to meet the need of all sinners for forgiveness and salvation. Jesus had received the ultimate endorsement of what he was doing from the Father who not only spoke that endorsement, but who also sent him "the Power from on High" that allowed him to fulfill the role of identifying with sinners, of being the Lamb of God bearing away sins.

Let us be clear about a few key points. Water baptism and Spirit Baptism are to be distinguished here. The former prepares for the latter; the latter confirms the submission to God's righteous will and plan expressed in the former. The Spirit alone anoints Jesus Christ and initiates the new age, just as we will see that the Spirit alone "christens" us and brings us into that age. The sequence of events from water baptism to Spirit Baptism is crucial. Water baptism is but preparatory for the Spirit, but also the shadow of which the Spirit is the substance. We will return to this point in our discussion of Christian baptism.

According to Luke, Jesus prays, probably for the Spirit (in view of John's words about Spirit Baptism). Henceforth in Luke, the Spirit is given in response to prayer (cf. 3:21 to 11:13; Acts 1:14 to 2:1-4; 2:21 and 2:39; 4:23-31, 8:15-17, and 22:16).[26] But perhaps we should associate this praying more with what precedes it (water baptism), than with what follows (Spirit Baptism). In a sense, water baptism as an act by ordinary and repentant Jews was an appeal to God for salvation in view of the nearness of redemptive-judgment. That is, it was a preparation for and an appeal for Spirit Baptism that would save, not destroy them.

For Jesus, too, it may be correct to say that his water baptism was an assumption of a role that required that he appeal to God to be equipped for that role. Thus, while his baptism was perhaps not in itself an appeal, it is closely linked to a "calling on the Name" in the Lukan account. This connection may be significant in view of later Christian practice. That we have said that in these narratives water baptism is but the symbolic shadow of Spirit Baptism should not be taken to mean that water baptism is of scant importance. Rather, as a sign or symbol of past and future redemptive-judgment (whether through water ordeals or through Spirit redemptive-judgment that is poured out like water), water baptism is very important. The close association of the symbol is not merely with purification, but with purification through redemptive-judgment and even death, and is one of the most significant themes developed by Paul in connection with baptism.

We have mentioned that Jesus himself likely saw his death as a baptism, probably because he saw in the symbolism of baptism by immersion a clear association not only with sinners or sin, but also with the sting of sin: death. He saw in baptism a sign of divine judgment, of the oath curse, of cutting off.[27] On that day, many were "buried" with John's baptism, but only Jesus arose from the waters and received the Spirit. As such, we may see a foreshadowing of Jesus' death and resurrection as a unique act. Further, it was only of Jesus that the voice spoke, "you are my beloved son with whom I am well pleased" (cf. Ps 2:7; Isa 42:1). But the words of Isaiah 42:1 do not stop there; they go on to say, "I have put my Spirit upon him, he will bring forth justice to the nations." Only as Jesus accepts this role in the act of water baptism can all righteousness be fulfilled.

SIGNS ON THE ROAD TO SACRAMENTS

At this point we must depart from the main stream of our discussion of baptism in the New Testament to deal with two key texts that Jeremias has called "presacramental." Neither of these texts speaks directly of water baptism or Spirit Baptism; they have often served, however, as ammunition for a certain view of water baptism. The first text is the beloved story of Jesus' blessing of the children in Mark 10:13ff. and parallels. Two things must be examined in this text: (1) What does it mean? (2) How does the gospel writer present what it means?

Parents and perhaps older children[28] were bringing younger children and even infants[29] (Luke 18:15) to Jesus so that he might "touch" them. Matthew explains that it was so that he might lay hands on them and pray for them. Conceivably Jesus was praying for something more than good health or blessing. Perhaps what he says after taking them reveals the content of his prayer, because it was the custom for parents to bring their children for blessing to rabbis on the Day of Atonement. Jeremias conjectures, plausibly, that this incident took place then.[30]

Perhaps reflecting a typical attitude that children were less mature and thus less important than adults and should not be allowed to bother Jesus, his disciples rebuked those bringing the children. This action produced a very surprising reaction in Jesus. He was extremely angry at his disciples. The verb ἠγανάκτησεν is found only in the Markan account of this story, and only here is it used of Jesus. It is a powerful and emotional word indicating that Jesus had strong feelings about the right of children to come and be in his presence. Jesus says to the disciples, "allow the children to come to me and do not hinder them for τῶν τοιούτων is the Kingdom of Heaven."[31]

The phrase τῶν τοιούτων, usually translated "of such," could mean one of three things: (1) such as these children, i.e., children are of the essence of the kingdom; (2) such as these = those adults who are like these children; (3) such as these = children of this sort who come or are brought to Jesus and those who are like them. Though some have argued that this phrase refers not to those particular children, nor all children, but perhaps to those who are childlike in character, this is not likely because, as Beasley-Murray remarks, "many normal occasions of the use of τοιοῦτος are intended to denote a class, of which the one mentioned in the context is an example. . . . It will be observed that . . . it is impossible to make the primary reference of τοιοῦτος a comparison with other individuals."

Further, what sense would it make for Jesus to be angry with the disciples for hindering children if he was only interested in those who were childlike in their faith or simplicity? Rather, a certain sort of child is said to belong to the kingdom (see number 3 in the previous paragraph)—those who come or are brought to Jesus, as well as those adults who are of this sort (willing to receive the kingdom as a child receives it). Beasley-Murray suggests that "this sort" refers to the fact that the children are the destined heirs of the kingdom (in the sense of Matt 5:2, 10).[32] While this interpretation is possible, it may also mean that the children of Jesus' disciples already have a place in the kingdom.

Many people at this juncture will wish to ask, as the Ethiopian eunuch once did, "What is to hinder (their) being baptized?" (Acts

8:36). If their place in the kingdom is granted already, how can the sign of that eschatological reality be refused? These questions need to be considered seriously, especially in view of the fact that Luke mentions that even infants are among those coming to Jesus who have a place in the kingdom.

At this point, however, the text says nothing directly about baptism, and some will argue that at most this text authorized some sort of infant blessing or dedication. Most of the church throughout history, however, has used this text as part of its infant baptismal service, and it is easy to see its emotional appeal. To Paedo-Baptists, Baptists are taking on the role of the recalcitrant disciples and hindering the "little ones" from coming to Jesus. Some might even repeat to Baptists the warning of the gospel: "Whoever receives one such child in my name receives me—but whoever causes one of those little ones who believe in me to stumble it would be better for him to have a great millstone fastened round his neck and to be drowned in the depth of the sea" (Matt 18:6). These are strong words not to be bandied about, for Matthew 18:6 refers to "believing little ones," which may include small children, but excludes infants.

A new twist has come into the discussion of Mark 10:13-16 and its parallels because of the research of Oscar Cullmann. He contends that this text was being used to justify infant baptism even by the time the evangelists were writing.[33] Cullmann argues that the verb κωλύω ("to hinder") had become a technical term used in connection with baptism. Further, this term was used in a ritual question, "What prevents this candidate from being baptized?" This claim gains plausibility when we note such texts as Acts 8:36, 10:47, 11:17, and even Matthew 3:13, where the discussion about baptism might be couched in traditional baptismal language by the gospel writer. Cullmann goes on to add that the use of the word κωλύω without any additional qualification is irregular, but that such irregularity is explained quite readily if a technical phrase is involved here.[34] He also notes that Luke may have deliberately mentioned the infants, and intimates that this text gave guidance on the baptism of "such as these."

In summary, Cullmann notes that the situation in Mark 10 very much resembles the baptism stories in Acts 10:47 and 11:17 in that all three have the following elements in common: (1) those who are to be blessed; (2) those who make the request for their blessing; (3) those who wish to reject the request; (4) the person who executes the blessing and firmly decides the admissibility and accepts the request; and (5) the formula "forbid them not."[35] To this Jeremias has added a lengthy chart involving several extrabiblical texts along with Matthew 18:3 and John 3:4 to show that the language of Mark 10:15 = Luke 18:17 is indeed the language of baptism and is a set formula.[36] He supports Cullmann's conclusions and notes that the mention of laying on of hands in Mark 10:16 and Matthew 19:15 may also be reminiscent of the baptismal rite.

How are we to evaluate these intriguing arguments? Beasley-Murray has argued that Luke's reference to infants is in fact a reference to small children, since this is the term used in Luke 18:16-17. This statement misses the whole point that the καί means "even" in Luke 18:15, which implies that the infants were also being brought in addition to other children. Jesus is depicted as simply using the general term to cover both infants and other children.

Furthermore, Luke 18:17 ("Whoever does not receive the Kingdom of God like a child shall not enter it") is a much-disputed verse. Are we to take "like a child" to refer to how we are to receive the kingdom, or should we translate it "as a child" to state when we are to receive it, or possibly "like a child" meaning that whoever does not receive the kingdom as he receives a child shall not enter it? The second option is entirely unlikely, especially since this saying is addressed to adults!

There is something to be said for the third option, as F. A. Schilling has shown.[37] For instance, the word translated "like" usually is used to liken two things to each other. Further, Mark 10:13-16, unlike Mark 9:33-37, is dealing with the nature of the kingdom, rather than how a disciple should behave in it, or receive it. Schilling concludes, "To be concerned about the Kingdom but to regard the child as trivial and unimportant is to miss the Kingdom, because it is of the essence of a child and must be accepted as a child is taken into a loving embrace."[38] If this is what Jesus is saying, then it is a most apt rebuke to disciples "hindering" children from coming to Jesus (and Beasley-Murray's argument falls to the ground). Schilling's view, however, is not the most likely in view of the focus of this pericope on: (1) how Jesus receives children; (2) the place children have in the kingdom, and (3) how disciples should receive the kingdom. Accordingly, the traditional view of this text is the most likely (ὅς probably links παιδία with ὅς ἄν).

Beasley-Murray's further objection that the verb κωλύω is often used in other ways than in a technical baptismal sense is not very significant.[39] The examples he cites (Mark 9:39; Luke 11:52; 1 Thess 2:16) have nothing to do with a context of baptism or blessing (as all Cullmann's references do). Further, it is no argument against a certain usage of a word that it is also used in other ways. The context, not the lexicon's statement about what it most often means, determines its usage. As Beasley-Murray himself admits,[40] there are indeed occurrences of the term *to hinder* in later Christian literature used in connection with baptism. Finally, I freely admit his objection to Jeremias's use of John 3:5 as a text that likely has no reference to baptism at all. This, however, in no way weakens Cullmann's arguments. Their strength is only a strength, however, if in fact infant baptism was being practiced when the gospels were written. This is a big "if" on which we cannot decide at this point.

The other pre-sacramental text that has often been the cause celebre of Paedo-Baptists is 1 Corinthians 7:14. In order to understand this text, we must set it in its context. Paul is giving advice to Christians, in this case those married to pagans. Apparently, there was some concern on the part of Christian spouses as to whether or not they could live with their pagan husbands/wives without becoming unclean or defiled in some way. In the midst of this advice to married Christians, Paul uses an argument to convince and reassure his readers that it was correct to continue living with their pagan spouses.

This argument concerns the state of children of religiously mixed marriages. We should note the sequence here: (1) a Christian spouse consecrates their non-Christian mate, whether husband or wife; (2) the children are not unclean, but holy or "clean," an important contrast. The converse of this would be if the Christian parent did not consecrate the spouse, then their children would be unclean.

Paul Jewett in an interesting argument maintains that *holy* here means "legitimate,"[41] and that when Paul says the unbeliever has been consecrated or sanctified he is referring to the marriage covenant by which the unbeliever has been consecrated and set apart for the exclusive fellowship of the believer. Numerous difficulties exist with this suggestion, which seems appealing at first. Paul says nothing about a bond of marriage sanctifying the unbeliever; rather, he says that the unbeliever himself is sanctified in the wife or (if the husband is the Christian) in the brother. Second, we must bear in mind that Paul is not talking about a marriage contracted between two Christians, but one contracted according to Greek customs and ideas, since at least one of the partners is a pagan. Biblical covenanting ideas do not apply here.

Indeed, it is likely that both were pagans at the time the marriage was undertaken, since the problem seems to have been created when one partner converted after the marriage and the birth of children. If, as seems likely, Paul is referring to a marriage contracted according to pagan customs, then it is impossible that he would appeal to the consecrating effect of that marital bond in view of Greek marriage practices. There was no idea of a covenant consecrating one partner to the other to the exclusion of all others. In fact, in Corinth as in Athens a man was allowed to have legal relations with concubines in addition to his citizen wife, and it was accepted practice for him to have relations with the famous "companions" without moral censure. Only the citizen-woman was restricted in her sexual relations. Further, Corinth was notorious for its sexual promiscuity.

It is inconceivable that Paul could be reassuring a Corinthian believer, particularly a woman, by saying, "do not worry, the original marriage covenant with its consecration to one partner has sanctified your relationship." In Corinth, the legitimacy of a child was determined solely by whether a married couple were both citizens, or whether a male citizen wished to legitimize a child by his concubine. Paul is not saying that this marriage is acceptable merely because it and its offspring are considered legitimate. Rather, Paul is appealing to an effect on a mixed marriage that a believing partner (or God through a believing partner) has on the marriage. Note the stress in the last clause of verse 14—νῦν δὲ ἅγιά ἐστιν ("but now it is holy"). Far from alluding to the sanctifying influence of the marital bond here, it is clear that while such a bond is allowable and made acceptable by the sanctifying influence of the believer, it is not more than allowable in contrast to a bond between two Christians (cf. 1 Cor 7:10-11 to v. 15). Thus, Jewett's interesting suggestion must be rejected and a solution must be sought elsewhere.

We seem to be in the context of some ideas about holiness that are not what we normally find in Paul (moral purity, being set apart for God) or what we today are familiar with, for it appears to involve the idea of holiness as something physically conveyed. Having said this, the idea of this sort of holiness is not completely isolated to this context in Paul. If we turn to Romans 11:16-18, we find a somewhat similar concept of holiness. Paul, in the midst of his argument about Israel and how their rejection has meant the reconciliation of the world, goes on to add:

> If the dough offered as first fruits is holy, so is the whole lump; and if the root is holy, so are the branches. But if some of the branches were broken off, and you, a wild olive shoot, were grafted in their place to share the richness of the olive tree, do not boast over the branches. If you do boast, remember it is not you that supports the root, but the root that supports you. (NRSV)

In the case of Romans 11:16-18, the lump and natural branches are clearly Israel and the ingrafted branches are Gentiles. But who or what is the root or first fruits? In the preceding verse, the argument has been that although Israel as a whole has rejected the Messiah and fallen away, yet there was a remnant that has not rejected God's plan for salvation. If these verses go with what precedes, then Paul is saying that there has always been a people of God, and there is now a remnant of Jews who remain righteous and believe in the Messiah (Paul, for instance). On the other hand, if these verses are to be seen as leading into the discussion that follows and relate to verse 28, then Paul may be referring to the patriarchs by the words "root" and "fruit." If the idea of firstness and origin is to be stressed, then the reference to the patriarchs is more likely.

Paul is not simply saying that the Gentiles have been joined to Jews who are Christians with a great heritage, but that the Gentiles have no reason to boast because they are grafted into Israel and into being heirs of Abraham. They owe a great deal to Israel and its forefathers. If this is so, then the text tells us a good deal about Paul's view of the covenant, that is, that there is in some sense a continuity between the old and new covenant, or, better said, a continuity between God's old covenant people and his new covenant people. The reason that Israel is still loved, though temporarily rejected by God, is because of their forefathers and the promises made to them. Their right relation to God and their holiness have sanctified an otherwise stubborn and rebellious lump. Here we see a sense of holiness on the basis of contact and relationship with one's forefathers. Note that this holiness did not prevent certain branches from being broken off. It is not a guarantee of salvation, but a gift that gives certain people a head start in their relationship with God—or stated another way, a special blessing and attitude of love and mercy from God originating from their forefathers and the promises made to them.

I submit that we have a similar concept of "holiness through relation" in 1 Corinthians 7:14. Here as well, the passage does not necessarily mean that the children are saved; rather, it places them in a position of special privilege or blessing in that God loves them and has mercy on them because of their Christian parents. There is perhaps a sense of these children being "set apart" (holy) for God because of their parents. That Paul is talking about covenantal holiness is likely since he is answering the question of whether or not one can be a member of Christ's holy body and be married to a nonholy unbeliever. This sort of holiness depends on relationships and need say nothing about moral purity. There is a difficulty with this view, however, in that Paul contrasts the uncleanness of a pagan with this holiness (1 Cor 7:14), which seems to imply a physical concept in both cases. We must investigate this further.

Jeremias notes that Paul is operating on a "household principle"— one believing member sanctifies the whole household. This idea is based on the idea of the corporate solidarity of the family, a sort of covenantal concept applied to the family.[42] Jeremias deduces rightly that this sort of holiness could apply to children with two Christian parents, as well as those with one. It is an argument about all children born in the church—or is it? What of those children born before the conversion of the parent(s)? Jeremias notes that the concept of holiness here is one based on Jewish ritual and the theology behind it. This interpretation is certainly likely, for in Judaism there was a distinction between children of proselytes born "not in holiness" (before the conversion of the parent) and those born after conversion who were "born in holiness" (*m. Ketub.* 4.3). Paul was probably relying on the language of Jews about proselytes and proselyte baptism, a language his converts in Corinth would be familiar with since they likely were converts from the synagogue fringe—that is, God-fearers and proselytes.

Thus, it is quite possible that Paul accepted their rules regarding whom it was administered t—children with their parents if they were born prior to conversion, but not to children born after conversion since they were "born in holiness." This would not exclude a later baptism if the child came to faith and requested it.[43] As Jeremias goes on to say, however, any good Jew knew that a child born in holiness would nonetheless receive a sign of the covenant on the eighth day after birth, that is, circumcision. Now, if Paul saw baptism as the replacement sign of the covenant for circumcision, then it is still possible that they might be baptized (this is a big "if" that can only be examined later in the discussion of Paul).

We can only say at this point that inasmuch as Paul's concept of holiness is related to his concept of covenantal continuity and also the unity of a family (even with only one Christian member) in some sort of consecration, it becomes conceivable that Paul might see baptism as a sign replacing that of circumcision.[44] Of course, it was Jesus' death and our spiritual circumcision that fulfill the significance of the old covenant sign. This distinction is important. As we shall see, the fact that a sign's significance is fulfilled in a theological reality in the new age does not rule out a continuity between two covenant signs as symbols, or between their mode of administration.

We must examine the objections to Jeremias's views at this point. First of all, Beasley-Murray rightly notes that it is not through baptism that children derive this holiness.[45] Further, he admits the fact that Paul is coalescing Jewish and Christian ideas here and in fact believes that Paul is applying the concepts of Romans 11:16ff. to this text.[46] He argues that it is illegitimate to distinguish between the holiness of the children and the fact that the unbelieving parent is "consecrated," since the word $\ddot{\alpha}\gamma\iota\sigma\varsigma$ is the root of both terms and since Paul is arguing that the husband is consecrated because the children are holy. If one is holy, the other must be holy, and if one is thereby accepted for baptism, so must the other. But is there no difference between a noun and a verb? Paul seems to be arguing as follows: "Your children are in a state of holiness because of the relationship to a believing parent. Therefore, the Christian parent must have some sort of consecrating effect on the parent who helped to produce this child, otherwise the unbelieving partner would defile the believer (in intercourse?) and the children that result from this union would be unclean."

Beasley-Murray does not bother to refute this view, but simply dismisses it.[47] He argues that it is not so much birth as belonging that matters in this text. Thus, we are talking about an effect of a relationship, not a result of being born of a Christian parent. He draws an analogy to 1 Peter 3:1ff. dealing with the effect of having a Christian wife in the house if she behaves in a certain manner. Here, however, there is no talk of a woman's behavior causing some effect; it is simply stated that she consecrates her partner. Paul says in 1 Corinthians 7:16 that the Christian partner might save or lead to salvation their mate; thus, he or she should not leave the family simply because the spouse is a pagan. Here there is some thought of the wife as a good example, and thus this concept is conceivably what Paul means in verse 14 as well. Beasley-Murray then points out that surely Paul would only be referring to a few children if he meant that it was children born after conversion who were holy, and what then of the majority of children born in unholiness? He argues that the reference to "your children" betrays no hint that it is limited to children one has had after conversion.[48]

These objections have real weight, but they overlook certain factors inherent in our context. For instance, Paul is addressing Christians who are concerned about their correct relationship with non-Christians. Their fear is that they or their children might be unclean in some sense because of contact, perhaps specifically sexual, with their mate. We know from such sayings as 1 Corinthians 7:1, where Paul likely is quoting what the Corinthians were arguing, that they were concerned about such sexual contacts. Paul (in 1 Corinthians 7:1-8) tries to allay their fears and prevent them from being so concerned about their sexual relations.

The specific concern of these Corinthian Christians seems to be about their relationship with their pagan mate and its fruits. When one realizes this, it becomes rather certain that in 1 Corinthians 7:14 Paul is referring only to children born of a Christian parent. Certainly, he is not saying that all children are holy. Paul betrays no hint of such modern notions as the innocence of all children. He is speaking specifically of a sanctifying influence that a Christian parent has. Presumably, he would have said that children born preconversion to a non-Christian were consecrated just as the pagan husband is. Perhaps he would have argued for their baptism. We simply cannot say on the basis of this text, since he is speaking only of a religiously mixed relationship and the children that resulted from it from the time when one partner converted to Christianity.

In conclusion, let us bring a few insights together. First, we noted that it is fairly certain that Paul's notion of holiness is derived from his Jewish background. This notion possibly derives from the concepts involved in Jewish proselyte baptism. If the latter is the case, then Paul might have argued for infant baptism on the basis of the analogy. Bear in mind that Paul treats even a mixed household as a unity in the sense that one holy member leavens the whole lump. We may add that this holiness is not a matter of moral purity, but of the power of the eschatological presence of the Holy Spirit operating through the believer.[49] This text, however, does not warrant maintaining that children of Christians are saved automatically, since Romans 11:16ff. reveals that one can be holy due to one's relation with one's forebears and still be a branch broken off from the covenant community. Perhaps *holy* means "set apart" for God, in which case it is but a small step from here to some sort of dedicatory rite of infants born into such a family.

That Paul contrasts *unclean* to *holy* could imply that holy is meant in a purely ceremonial sense. But I believe that Gentile Corinthians were not so much concerned with ceremonial defilement as with spiritual or moral defilement since they prided themselves on being "spiritual" Christians. Further, the term *holy* here appears to include the idea of cleanness but goes beyond it in a positive direction. The reassurance that Paul offers the Corinthians is not merely that believers can have clean relationships with an unbeliever, but that through God's grace working in them they can have a positive and sanctifying influence on their family. The believer is God's agent for good and for blessing in a mixed family, and the children and spouse of such a believer receive a special added benefit through this believer. Through the Christian, the non-Christian family in some sense experiences the power of Christ—his love and mercy. As such, the family may be saved through this sanctifying influence (1 Cor 7:16), but this is not automatic. Paul's questions in 1 Corinthians 7:16 refer to a possibility. Only the children are said to be in the state of holiness, and Beasley-Murray is right that these could only be infants since the Corinthians had not been Christians for long.[50] Perhaps this was a generally recognized assurance given to parents in mixed marriages that their children were set apart for God, for Paul appeals to something axiomatic, something the Corinthians already had been told.

In any case, one can distinguish between a consecrating effect that a believer has on an adult, and the state of holiness of the infants of Christian parents. That this is a matter of importing modern ideas about influence into the text should not be suggested, because the idea of the conveying of holiness or cleansing or healing through contact (even physical contact) with a source of holiness or power is one that is found in various places in the New Testament (cf. Mark 5:28-30 and its parallels, Acts 19:11-12, and Acts 5:15). If holiness meant for Paul what it meant for a Jew in this instance, then their children were within the covenant community. This was a blessing they could later reject by opting out of the community and being limbs broken off. For now, however, God, in his grace, had given them a place "for the sake of their forefathers" (Rom 11:28), or in this case because of the Christian partner. This text cannot tell us clearly whether or not Paul accepted infant baptism. It does reveal, however, that he had a covenantal concept of holiness which he applied to the family, as a comparison of Romans 11:16ff. and 1 Corinthians 7:14 reveals. No more can be said at this point. We must turn now to Acts and examine what Luke has to tell us about the beginnings of the Christian practice of baptism.

Chapter 3

PARTING THE WATERS

The Beginnings of Water Baptism as a Christian Rite— The Acts of the Apostles

In the beginning of our discussion, we mentioned that a great deal of weight has been placed on various texts in Acts to argue strongly for a certain normative practice or theology in regard to the relation of Spirit Baptism and water baptism. Further, certain other texts in Acts (household texts; Acts 2:39; etc.) have been used to argue for infant baptism. There are some difficulties with both kinds of approach to Acts, precisely because they jump the hermeneutical gun. It is one thing to have a descriptive account of a baptism in Acts from which we may deduce how the rite was performed on some occasion. It is quite another to say that this practice is prescriptive or normative.

Luke is deliberately selective in Acts, and thus some of the descriptive statements are meant to be examples not only of how things were done, but also presumably of how they should be done. However, in many narratives Luke intends no such thing; indeed, he intends precisely to warn against certain examples (such as the case of Simon Magus, or Ananias and Sapphira).

Thus, we must tread cautiously through these texts, looking for repeated positive patterns before we may begin to talk of normal practices, much less normative ones. A further important point is that Acts is a self-confessed missionary document. It would be surprising then to find more than a hint of a solution to second-generation problems or to find any discussion of examples of baptism that do not involve Jews and Gentiles entering the community from the outside. Such is the nature of a missionary document about Christian beginnings. From the very genre of Acts we should not expect to find infant baptism unless it is the baptism of infants as members of a whole household that enters the church. Accordingly, we briefly examine Matthew 28:19-20 before turning to Acts 2:39, the household baptism texts, and various other key passages.

MATTHEW 28: GREAT COMMISSION (OR OMISSION?)

When Jesus commanded his followers to go and make disciples of all nations (Matt 28:19-20), he spoke of two things in which they would be involved. In the Greek, both activities are subordinate to the main verb *to make disciples* and explain how it is to be done: (1) Baptizing in the name of the Father, Son, and Holy Spirit; and (2) teaching them all Jesus had commanded his followers to do. We note that Jesus not only commanded this, he also gave the community of his followers the authority to carry it out. This fact is evident because the command to make disciples follows and is dependent upon Jesus' statement that all authority had been given to him. Therefore (οὖν), he delegated some of that authority to his followers to carry out a mission to τὰ ἔθνη (probably to all nations, though it could mean to all the Gentiles). From the inception of Christian baptism, then, as envisioned by the First Evangelist, it was to be an act performed by Jesus' community, under his authority, in (or into) God's name as part of the process of making disciples.

There is no intimation here of baptism being anything other than a community act, for the main verb says what the baptizers are to do—

make disciples, baptizing and teaching. It says nothing of what the baptized are to do: profess faith, confess sins. This text gives no justification for Karl Barth's frequent assertion that water baptism is to be the first ethical act of a new believer in which he commits himself to God. Interestingly Matthew 28:19-20 is the only statement that we have anywhere about the real beginnings of specifically Christian baptism as initiated by Christ.

Jesus speaks first of water baptism and then of teaching as the essence of making disciples. I assume that Jesus is not commanding Spirit Baptism since that is a purely divine act for which the community can only pray. Such a divine act could not be commanded of the community. Of course, this may tell us nothing about a proper order of initiation, but conceivably the text might be intended in that direction. This order is, after all, part of a command to the community, not merely a descriptive statement. We can deduce from this statement, however, that Jesus saw water baptism as an important part of making disciples. Baptism is part of a command to missions; it is an essential part of missionary work.

Jesus, however, gives no inkling here of what his views about the baptizing of his followers' children might be. If this is all Jesus said to his disciples about water baptism as an act of the post-resurrection community, and we have no reason to think otherwise, then it appears that the idea of baptism being a two-way act (divine/human or community/individual), much less being primarily a one-way act from the side of the baptized after catechesis, must have its origins in later tradition. In Matthew 28:19-20 it is viewed as an act of the community in the authority of Jesus. Whatever else the apostles deduced about Christian baptism likely came from the influence of John's baptism or perhaps even Jewish proselyte baptism or circumcision.

ALL IN THE FAMILY? ACTS 2:39

When we were discussing Jesus' baptism we noted that it was the anointing of the Spirit that ushered in the sequence of eschatological events, for it was this that equipped Jesus for ministry as Representative, as Lamb of God, and as Servant. Dunn says, "Jesus' ministry as Servant and Representative is consummated by his suffering the messianic baptism of fire on behalf of his people."[1] Jesus had to enter the New Age first by baptism in Spirit, and then by providing a means for others to enter it by himself, undergoing a baptism of fire on the cross. Only subsequent to this could Jesus fulfill what John had said of him: that he would baptize with Holy Spirit. In fact, not until his utter triumph in his exaltation to the Father's right hand could Jesus send the Spirit that ushered his followers into the New Age. In Luke-Acts, Pentecost is clearly the watershed for Jesus' followers. It brings to a climax all that had come before, and it is rightly seen as the birthday of the church. The fact that John 20:22 may record this event in a different way should not lead us astray.

In the first place, I doubt whether John meant to inform us that Jesus actually gave the Spirit when he met in private with his disciples at his first appearance in Jerusalem to the Eleven. The event that follows this narrative in the Fourth Gospel shows no change in the disciples' behavior, nor have they begun the mission to which Jesus commissioned them in John 20:21. Nor are we to think of two gifts of the Spirit, one in John 20 and one in Acts 2.[2] Even in the Gospel of John, Jesus made clear that he would have to go away before another Comforter could come (cf. John 14:15-17, 15:26, 16:7) though some have thought this may refer to Jesus' death rather than His ascension into heaven. What we may have in John 20:22 is: (1) a symbolic prophetic sign act by which Jesus assured the inner circle of disciples that the Spirit would come to them and give them the power to do what Jesus gave them the authority to do, or (2) simply John's different way of portraying Pentecost as an event that happened to Jesus' disciples. The former view makes much more sense of John's gospel as well as of Acts. In any case, Pentecost is not simply a second stage of Spirit endowment.

Only at Pentecost is Joel's prophecy fulfilled that relates specifically to the inbreaking of the new and eschatological age upon the human sphere. This is clear, as Dunn has rightly shown. How then does Acts 2:38-39 fit into this picture?[3] One factor about Pentecost that is often overlooked is that it is the beginning of the new covenant for Jesus' disciples. For Luke, the Spirit is given as the Promise (cf. Luke 24:49; Acts 1:4; 2:33, 38)—the covenant promise of God to his people (cf. Acts 2:39; 7:17; 13:23, 32; 26:6; cf. Rom 4:13, 16, 20; 9:8; Gal 3:14).

It appears that Luke, perhaps following Paul, equates the blessing of Abraham with the gift of the Spirit (cf. Gal 3:14). How so? The wording of Acts 2:39 clearly alludes to Genesis 12:7-10 and the Abrahamic covenant of promise (cf. Acts 3:25). Acts 2:38 identifies the covenant promise with the gift of the Spirit, and Acts 2.39 repeats the promise given to Abraham, "the promise is to you and to your children." Thus, the gift of the Spirit is not only the necessary and sufficient means by which one becomes a Christian, but also the means whereby anyone may enter into the blessing of Abraham. Through the receiving of the Spirit, all the nations of the earth (which is possibly alluded to by "all who are far off" in Acts 2:39, though cf. below) are blessed. When Abraham heard this promise he had as yet no children, but Peter's audience of Jews likely did. Thus, while "your children" might mean your future descendants (as it did initially with Abraham), this is unlikely its primary meaning in Acts 2:39.

Beasley-Murray agrees that this verse likely refers primarily to present children, as Joel's prophecy referred to your sons and daughters prophesying (2:17). What then is being said here? The promise of God applies not only to Peter's Jewish listeners, but also to their progeny. I submit that this is a clear example of the household principle that we see in Paul. Note, however, that this statement is being spoken to Jews to whom the promise was given originally. Thus, it could be argued that it is simply a fulfillment of the old covenant promise to the old covenant people in an old covenant household way. It might be argued further that there is no mention of the progeny of those who are "far off," which might imply that they receive the promise on a different basis. This overlooks the fact that the Spirit ushers in the New Age.

If it is being said that they receive the promise on the basis of the household principle, then at the least for Jews the household principle still applies in the New Age. The promise to Abraham is being enacted along the lines of the Old Testament covenantal approach to the family. And what of the meaning of *all who are far off?* Is it a reference to those who are spatially far off, or to those who are far off in time (that is, future generations)? The parallels to the text in Genesis 12:7-10 might suggest that the far off are the nations of the earth, not represented in Jerusalem on "that day." An examination of the larger context in Acts, however, suggests otherwise.

Is it likely that Peter—who required a revelation from God to send him to Cornelius's house and even a further confirmation from the Spirit to perform the breakthrough which let the Jerusalem council know that salvation had come to the Gentiles (see Acts 10:9-47)—would have announced on Pentecost that the promise was also to the far-off Gentile nations or peoples? Notice that in 10:34 Peter declares the new insight he has as a result of his vision and revelation through the Spirit: "Truly I perceive that God shows no partiality, but in every nation anyone who fears him." Only after God had revealed to Peter that the Gentiles were not unclean could he understand that in every nation anyone who fears God is acceptable. Further, the text also says (10:45) that Peter was amazed because even the Gentiles received the Spirit.

I submit that Peter could not possibly have been referring to the Gentile people or nations as "all those who are far off" in Acts 2:38-39. Two possibilities remain. Peter is referring to the Diaspora Jews who are far off, or to those who are far off in time (future generations). Though many scholars would see here a reference to Diaspora Jews, they overlook the fact that Luke stresses in 2:8-11 that Diaspora Jews representing countries from all over the Mediterranean were present, not far off, and heard Peter's message on that day. Further, Acts 2:39 appears to distinguish between those present ("you" and, possibly "your children") and those absent (all who are far off). Thus, I conclude that it is more likely that in context Peter is referring to future generations, not far-off Gentile peoples or Diaspora Jews who were in fact present and represented in number on that day in Jerusalem. If this assertion is correct, then certain things follow from it.

Those adults who heard Peter and also those who read Peter's words as part of the Pentecost message to the church are warranted in believing that the promise is made to the parents, children, and their future generations, even though at this point only the immediate listeners (or readers) are called to repent and be baptized. It is effectively a promise to the parents that God will also make to the children, though they are not yet able to receive it. Indeed, they may not yet be born, being "far off" in time.

At this point in the argument Beasley-Murray points out that the promise is for everyone whom the Lord calls (2:39). He goes on to say, "That presumes a call to which a response is made, for the prophecy of Joel is still being quoted . . . 'for in Mount Zion and in Jerusalem there shall be those who escape as the Lord has said, and among the survivors shall be those whom the Lord calls' (Joel 2:32)."[4] I can understand why Beasley-Murray would point this out if the text of either Joel or Acts or Genesis 12 spoke of the promise being for those who call on the name of the Lord. None of these three texts reads that way, however. In our text, the emphasis is on God's election and the fact that the promised Spirit is a divine promise and gift as is evident in Acts 2:1ff. Of course, the call and promise must be responded to, but the divine initiative precedes the response. There is no mention of prayer in Acts 2:1-12, only a gathering upon which the Spirit falls. In this context, after the miracle of Pentecost, Peter explains what has happened and preaches the gospel so that people will understand properly what has already happened and will respond to the promise and the manifestation of the fulfillment of the promise at hand (Acts 2:14-26).

God's promise and his call, as well as his gift of the promise in the initial miracle at Pentecost, all precede any response. Also, however, Peter calls his listeners to respond to the divine initiative as it is manifested in the coming of the Spirit and the preaching of the gospel, in the following fashion: "Repent and be baptized everyone of you in the name of Jesus Christ for the forgiveness of sins and you shall receive the gift of the Holy Spirit." We have noted the affinities this has with John the Baptizer's preaching and practice, so that already we see a combination of Christ's institution with the disciples' background knowledge of other baptismal practices. What is interesting is the sequence here: call to repentance, baptism, and the promise of the Spirit. In this initial case, no mention is made of prior confession of sins or profession of faith, simply the act of repentance and presumably submission to water baptism (being an outward indication of that repentance in adults).

But if, as Dunn says (I believe he is right) the reception of the Spirit is the beginning of Christian experience and entrance into the church (the new covenant, the New Age), then water baptism must be seen as still a preparatory act for the future eschatological gift, as it was in the case of John's baptism. If there is an approved pattern to be derived from this text, it is water then Spirit, or even repentance-water-Spirit, but not Spirit reception then water baptism. We have seen that water baptism is used as a vehicle of repentance or of the beginnings of a faith response to the gospel. If someone objects that one cannot exercise faith without grace going before, then I agree. But it should be remembered that the Holy Spirit may convey grace that leads to repentance and faith before the Spirit confers himself in response to these things.

The significance of Acts 2:39 does not end with these matters, however, for in the Western text there is a very interesting variation of the standard text. As is recognized generally, the Western text of Acts 2:17 and 2:39 was altered by a change from a second to a third plural pronoun (2:17), and from the second to the first plural pronoun (2:39), so that Peter's words would apply not only to his Jewish listeners but also to the Gentiles in 2:17, and to Christians instead of Jews in 2:39.[5] The effect of this change is interesting for our discussion because it implies that the promise is now referred to Christians and their children. Thus, the household principle is made to apply to Christians.

Further, recall that the Western text reads: "Be baptized for the promise is to us and our children." This statement may imply that when this textual change was made there was already in the church baptism of children (perhaps even infants, though τέκνον usually means child). This change probably is to be dated about A.D. 150.[6] If this change is meant to support infant baptism, then it is our earliest extrabiblical (extracanonical) evidence for infant baptism. The crucial point is that the phrase *you and your children* may be a reproduction of a stereotyped formula—the household formula. This is more likely if Acts 2:39 is following Joel 2:28-29, for it reads: "Your sons and your daughters . . . your young men and your old men . . . even your men servants and maid servants," which is clearly a paraphrase for the family in its completeness.[7] This line of thought leads us to ask whether other texts give evidence of a household principle in relationship to the act of water baptism. Several possible candidates are Acts 11:14, 16:15, 16:32-34, 18:8, and 1 Corinthians 1:16. We must examine these texts at this juncture.

A HOUSEHOLD NAME: HOUSEHOLD BAPTISM TEXTS?

By way of introduction to these passages, it will prove useful to determine whether or not there is evidence for a household formula in the Old Testament. Ethelbert Stauffer concluded after a study of the Old Testament evidence that the phrase "so and so's household or whole household" refers specifically to one's progeny.[8] Jeremias updated these arguments and maintains that when the whole household is mentioned no single member is left out.[9] He shows that it is impossible to restrict the word *all* or *whole* to the household slaves for, as Philemon 10 and 16 and Aristides, *Apology* 15.6 reveal, servants were encouraged by their owners to become Christians sometime after their masters had converted.[10]

Jeremias then provides a wealth of evidence from secular Greek usage and the papyri that οἶκος meant family including children (Hesiod, Pindar, Plato, and the tragic poets). But this, as Jeremias admits, gives little help in regard to biblical usage. He then turns to the Old Testament evidence for the formula "he and his household," or "he and his whole household" and in fact the evidence is abundant (Gen 7:1, 36:6, 45:8, 47:12, 50:7f.; Deut 6:22; 1 Sam 1:21, 9:20, 22:15-16; 2 Sam 6:11, 21, 9:9, 15:16, and Judg 16:31). In most, if not all, of these examples, the intention is that everyone in the family be included. The phrase is found in both secular and cultic contexts. Especially interesting are such texts as Genesis 18:19; 1 Samuel 2:30; Deuteronomy 25:9; 1 Chronicles 10:6; Numbers 18:1; Genesis 46:31, 47:12; and Judges 16:31, where the term *house* refers solely or primarily to one's progeny. In fact, Jeremias says that there is no passage in the Old Testament where one can find the term *house* restricted by the nature of the term to its adult male and female members.[11]

The inclusion of children in the term is taken for granted. While Jeremias has also found impressive evidence in the Old Testament Apocrypha and elsewhere for its continued use in the intertestamental period, it is not found in Philo or Josephus. Further, in only one example from this period is the formula connected with circumcision (*Jub.* 15:24). Thus, the evidence for an Old Testament background for this phrase is impressive, though its intertestamental usage is less so. What then of the evidence of the early church literature? Interestingly, in the *Shepherd of Hermas: Vision* 1.3.1 and 2 (cf. *Herm. Vis.* 11.2.3 and 3.1) *house* means specifically one's children. The term is thus used in the early church in this way.

In the canonical gospels, John 4:53 is perhaps the one occasion where the household formula is expanded so that we are told specifically who is included in the phrase. Here we are told of the healing of the official's son. When the official realized that his son had been healed at the moment Jesus had spoken, we are told that he believed— and all his household. Presumably then, the son was also old enough to believe, and the word *household* includes him. One could construe this verse so that all the household equals all those old enough to believe, in which case infants, if present, would not be included in the formula. Thus, the evidence of this verse is ambiguous.

Did then Luke or the early church use this phrase in the same way it was used in the Old Testament and in the early church? In Acts 11:14

Peter is reporting to the Jerusalem church about the conversion of Cornelius and his family. He recounts how he was sent "by revelation" (in conjunction with the arrival of messengers) to Cornelius's house. The angel had spoken to Cornelius and told him, "Send to Joppa and bring Simon called Peter; he will declare to you [singular] a message by which you and all your household will be saved." The story continues, "As I began to speak, the Holy Spirit fell on them (ἐπ' αὐτούς). . . . If then God gave them (αὐτοῖς) the same gift as he gave us when we believed in the Lord Jesus Christ, who was I that I could withstand God?"

Let us refer back to the other account of this story in 10:44ff.: "[T]he Holy Spirit fell on all who heard the Word." Peter responds: "Can anyone forbid water for baptizing these people who have received the Holy Spirit just as we have?" The first item of importance is that in Acts 11:14 the angel is addressing Cornelius as an individual but refers to the salvation of all his household. The story shifts into the plural when it speaks of those upon whom the Spirit fell. The previous account of the story must not be divorced from this one, for here we are told that the Holy Spirit fell not on the whole house, but on those who heard the word. Further, Peter speaks of the baptism of those who received the Spirit—those who heard the word.

I deduce that only those who heard the word and received the Spirit were baptized, for only they are referred to as no longer having impediments to their water baptism. This does not mean necessarily that the household phrase in 11:14 refers only to those who could hear and receive the Spirit, nor does it mean necessarily that there were no infants in the household. Both of these things are possible, but if Acts 2:38-39 is any guide, what we have is the promise being extended to Cornelius and his progeny on the basis of the household principle. One must be old enough to hear and receive the word and promised Spirit, but God's promise precedes our ability to respond. In short, this angel's message may have reassured Cornelius about infant salvation until they receive the Spirit, but it gives no warrant for the assumption that infants received water baptism (as Acts 10:47 shows). In fact, it intimates the opposite.

Before turning to the next household text, we should note that in terms of an order of baptism here, we have Spirit then water. Only when Cornelius and those with him believed did they receive the Spirit; the Spirit was not some later gift, but part of the event of conversion.[12] The order here, as it is in Paul, is commitment to the Word resulting in God's gift of the Spirit. One cannot separate the act of faith from Spirit Baptism by any significant length of time (cf. 10:43, 11:17, 13:7 on God's response to saving faith). In this case, it was necessary for God to bear witness to the Gentile conversion in a dramatic demonstration of Spirit Baptism so that Peter and the other Jewish Christians would be able to have no more doubts about their place in the people of God. One thing is clear in this text: once a person has the reality of Spirit Baptism in his life, then there can be no reason for not giving him the symbol of God's divine redemptive-judgment—that is, water baptism—immediately, regardless of the age. The order of Spirit-water, especially if separated by a significant time interval, could never be normative, since Peter sees something distinctly wrong with someone who has the Spirit and yet has not received water baptism. More on this later.

Let us now turn to another household text, Acts 16:30ff. This is the familiar story of the Philippian jailor who awakes with a start to find the jail doors open and Paul still sitting there. After this amazing fact and its implications dawn on the jailor, he brings Paul and Silas out of the jail and asks them, "Men, what must I do to be saved?" The reply is, "Believe in the Lord Jesus and you [singular] will be saved; you and your household (σὺ καὶ ὁ οἶκός σου)." We are told that Paul and Silas then spoke the word of the Lord to him and all of those in his house, and he was baptized immediately with all his family. Unless we find it here or in another household text, there is clearly no precedent for vicarious faith in the gospel. I do not believe the jailor's household was saved by his individual faith.

We are told specifically that Paul and Silas spoke the word to all who were in Cornelius's house, which presupposes that only adults or children who could receive such a message were present. Perhaps it is important that we do not have in this passage the phrase *all the household,* which might refer specifically to small children. Rather, we are told of *your household* and *all who were in his house.* I conclude from this that the expression "you and your household" could be used to refer to a family that did not have infants. This is only what one would expect; but let it be said that the phrase *your house* includes "all who were in the house." The formula thus means the family in its entirety; however, there were no infants in this instance.

What Luke probably means in Acts 16:31 is this: "Believe in the Lord Jesus, you and your household, and you and your household will be saved." No mention is made here of the promised Spirit, or the effects of Spirit Baptism. We are told only that there was an exhortation to faith and that the jailor believed. The focus is on him, but note that he and his household rejoiced in this conversion, implying that they all believed and received God's Spirit (which stirs up such joy). Once again, we find the household principle of inclusion into the new community, but this household included no little ones. Further, water baptism followed immediately after the gospel was preached to the family. There is no hint of any lengthy catechetical teaching, though perhaps there was some confession or profession involved, or the Spirit evidenced conversion in some way. We may have the order Spirit then water here, but it is difficult to tell. If so, the "immediately" tells us that any appreciable interval after receiving Spirit Baptism or giving evidence of belief is ruled out.

Another text involving household baptism is Acts 16:11-15, where we find the story of Lydia, the seller of purple goods. She was a God-fearer who prayed with others who followed Jewish practices (11:13-14). We are told only of her conversion, but we are told of the baptism of her and her household (11:15). The crucial factors in this text are as follows: (1) Lydia was a business woman of some means; (2) she was not at her house when she was converted, but at the river at a place of prayer; (3) she had gathered with other women at this place; (4) she and her household were baptized at the river before they returned to the house, so they must have accompanied her to the prayer meeting.

Though we are told only of Lydia's faith, her household was baptized also, once again witnessing the practice of maintaining family unity in baptism. But who was included in this unity? If Lydia was a widow, then she probably did not have small children or infants. In any case, we are told only of women, not children or infants, assembling at the river, which probably involves female relatives, slaves, and possibly older children of Lydia. Thus, we must conclude that while this text is evidence for family solidarity in baptism, it is improbable that there were infants included in that solidarity at the river. Further, we have yet another instance of belief followed immediately by water baptism. If the phrase *the Lord opened her heart* refers to God's gift of the Spirit, then we have an incident of the order Spirit then water (cf. Luke 24:45 where a similar phrase does not seem to refer to Spirit Baptism, but is nonetheless some sort of enlightenment by the Lord, a divine act).

Acts 18:8 relates the story of a conversion of a prominent synagogue leader in Corinth named Crispus. The reference is brief and to the point: Crispus believed in the Lord with the whole of his house (σὺν ὅλῳ τῷ οἴκῳ αὐτοῦ), and many Corinthians, hearing, believed and were baptized. Whether we are being told of the baptism of some Corinthians besides Crispus and his household, or including them, is not completely clear. It is likely the latter. The text is clear in saying that Crispus believed with his whole household, meaning that they believed as well. Once again, the principle of household inclusion is obvious, but do we have a reference to infants? Would Luke assert that infants believed with Crispus and were baptized?

In this case then, the modifier "whole" is present, yet it is unlikely there were infants here. We must either conclude that the household formula still implies the entire family but that no infants are involved, or that Luke is using the phrase "the whole house" in a general way (in which case there is no household formula). The former seems more probable, and once again we note the connection of faith and water baptism for the household. There was no delay in baptizing any who could believe and receive, nor is there any mention of a probational or catechetical period for Crispus's children (if any).

Finally, we turn to the one use of the οἶκος phrase outside Acts that relates to baptism—1 Corinthians 1:16. Paul says that he baptized the house(hold) of Stephanas (Στεφανᾶ οἶκον). Paul also operated on the principle of household inclusion; however, again we do not know who was included in the house of Stephanas. The only other reference we have to this family is 1 Corinthians 16:15, which speaks of the οἰκίαν Στεφανᾶ. They are said to be the first converts in Corinth and "they have devoted themselves to the service of the saints." It is impossible that Paul is speaking of converted infants who served the church.

What may we conclude about the household formula in the New Testament? First, there are no clear cases where infants might be involved or referred to by such a formula. Moreover, the two accounts of the Cornelius story specifically exclude the possibility of infants being baptized even if they were part of the family. I see no reason that the phrase *his (whole) household* cannot mean the family in its entirety, as Jeremias contends; however, I find no evidence in the texts he cites for infants being present or, if present, being baptized. I do find evidence in Acts 11:14ff. that God's promise extended to Cornelius's progeny (as in Acts 2:38-39), but promise given and promise received are not synonymous.

I also find in these texts a clear indication of the close connection of faith and water baptism, and in some cases Spirit Baptism is clearly connected to these two as well. We learn little or nothing about a normative order of initiation (including water baptism, Spirit baptism, profession of faith, etc.) from these texts. We do learn that if someone has the Spirit, then water baptism should not be delayed. We conclude that those who are searching for hints of infant baptism in the New Testament would do well to look elsewhere than among the household texts. We could also ask whether the inclusion of households into the community of faith is a missionary principle (tactic of God's emissaries), or a reflection of the divine mercy of God who does not wish to break up a family when the gift of salvation is poured out on them.

PHILIP GETS HIS FEET WET: ACTS 8:4-40

Perhaps the most puzzling incident in Acts that relates to our discussion is in Acts 8, the conversion of the Samaritans and Simon Magus. This story certainly reveals that water baptism must not be confused with Spirit Baptism, nor are they necessarily two sides of one coin (one event). Rather, they are two parts of the process of conversion. For many if not most, conversion is more of a process than an event, as one would expect from Matthew 28:19-20, where making disciples is clearly a process over a period of time involving the act of water baptism and a period of teaching. Acts 8 makes plain that water baptism, whatever its virtues, does not make a person a Christian.

The story's principle character, Simon the sorcerer, amazed the nation of Samaria (8:9) with his magic (8:11), and thus his reputation was widespread and affected a large number of people (8:16). Into this atmosphere of superstition and longing for spiritual power came Philip preaching Christ to the Samaritans. They "gave heed" to him for two reasons: (1) because of what he said, and (2) because of the miracles he performed (healing, exorcizing, cf. 8:6-7). It was perhaps unfortunate that these mighty deeds happened among these superstitious Samaritans, for it appears that he engendered a sort of miracle-working type of faith that was by no means a saving faith. The eschatological expectations of the Samaritans during this time are well attested, and John 4 as well as Josephus bear witness to them.[13] In such a heated atmosphere, that Philip, like Simon, drew a crowd is not surprising. The Samaritans apparently were expecting some sort of Messiah figure in connection with certain awaited events at Mount Gerizim. Thus, when Philip preached the coming of the "Anointed One," it may well have been that they interpreted this preaching in terms of their own expectations and accepted it on those terms.

The text tells us that "when they believed Philip as he preached the good news about the Kingdom of God and the name of Jesus Christ, they were baptized both men and women. Even Simon believed, and after being baptized he continued with Philip" (8:12-13). The Spirit, however, did not fall upon the Samaritans after they believed and were baptized.[14] Evidence that something was wrong is clear from Simon's behavior recorded in verses 18ff., where he tries to buy the power of giving the Holy Spirit. Peter rightly sees that Simon is not converted, and says to him, "May your money perish with you! You have no part or share in this word,[15] because your heart is not right before God. Repent of this wickedness and pray to the Lord. . . . For I see you are full of bitterness and captive to sin" (8:21-23). This is not a description of a Christian who simply lacks certain charismatic gifts.

Further, Simon is not said to have heeded Peter's advice. We are told that, being afraid, he asked Peter to pray that these things would not happen. From first to last he is unconverted, though he obviously believed in the power to which Philip, Peter, and John had access. Though the verbal form of πίστις is ascribed to Simon, as it was of the other Samaritans, this does not necessarily imply they had saving faith. The word can mean intellectual assent or recognition, rather than commitment to God or saving trust, and in fact there are other instances of this usage in Acts.[16] We are not told that these Samaritans believed in the Lord, rather it is said they believed in Philip! Though they were like Simon in this regard, they went on to receive the Holy Spirit (v. 17), while Simon did not, as far as we know.

What conclusions may we draw from this text about water baptism? First, even some sort of confession of faith is no assurance that a candidate has saving faith or is worthy of water baptism. Philip obviously did not investigate very far into what the Samaritans believed, and once again we see reason to doubt whether or not there was any set of catechetical questions or set confession of faith required in order to receive water baptism at this stage in church history. Probably, Philip preached, made an appeal that those who wished to align themselves with the name of Jesus and his kingdom should repent and be baptized, and then he baptized whoever came forth. We have here the order water then Spirit, with a considerable gap between the two. The irregularity of the situation probably means that we should not place too much stress on the gap between the two baptisms.

Immediately following this incident is the story of the Ethiopian eunuch (8:26-40), which involves this same Philip (cf. Acts 6:5). Here we have the conversion of an African God-fearer who would have been given an inferior place in much of the religious activity of Judaism because he was a eunuch. This fact, however, does not hinder Philip, who explains Isaiah 53 to the eunuch and uses it as a springboard to preach Christ (8:35). Possibly Philip was aware of some of the connections made by Jesus and/or John about Jesus' baptism and death and his role as Servant of the Lord, and that water baptism as a symbol came naturally into the conversation from the discussion of Jesus as the Servant of Isaiah 53.

Once again, after Philip's teaching we have a baptism, but in this case the eunuch himself requests it, and his question may reflect the fact that something was hindering him from receiving Jewish proselyte baptism. Philip complies with the request, and they both descend into the river for baptism by immersion.[17] As the two men came out of the water, Philip was caught up by the Spirit, and so probably was the eunuch since it is said that he went on his way rejoicing (cf. 8:8 and 16:34). Dunn is right that, like Jesus' experience, the Spirit descended not as the head of the baptized rose above the water, but as he climbed out of the river. Thus, we are not free to see Spirit Baptism as part of water baptism. Again we have the order water then Spirit in close succession, the former being preparatory for receiving the Spirit and a truly Christian experience. As is well known, the Western text at a later date has added verse 37, probably because at some point it was felt necessary to show that the eunuch made a profession of faith. Thus, it reads, "'If you believe with all your heart you may.' And he replied, 'I believe that Jesus Christ is the Son of God.'"[18]

THE DISCIPLES OF JOHN: ACTS 18-19

Before we examine Paul's conversion, we must first pause to note two texts in Acts 18 and 19 that relate something about those who had contact with John the Baptizer and his teaching. John A. T. Robinson long ago put his finger on one of the weaker but frequently used assumptions in New Testament scholarship when he remarked that no evidence is available to support the common view that the Baptizer's followers were at odds with or competing with Christians for followers.

Indeed, Jesus' relation to John in the gospels is uniformly friendly, and the Fourth Evangelist even records that John the Baptizer told his followers to expect that his own friends might leave him to be with Jesus (cf. John 3:25-30).[19] It is probably wrong to see a polemic against John and his followers in the New Testament. I do not agree with Robinson that John did not continue to have a group of followers for several decades after his death. Acts 19:1ff. seems to make clear that he did. What are we to make of these people who had a connection with John?

In Acts 18:24-28 Apollos is said to have known only the baptism of John. In this, Apollos was like the twelve disciples in 19:3. It is interesting that both are in Ephesus at the same time, but beyond this Luke is careful to distinguish Apollos from the twelve disciples. Too much exegesis of Acts 18:24-28 has assumed that Apollos was not yet a Christian simply because the twelve disciples had not heard of or received the Holy Spirit. As Kirsopp Lake remarks about Luke, "He does not regard the Ephesians as disciples or deny that Apollos was a Christian."[20]

Apollos is distinguished from the Twelve in the following ways: (1) Apollos is not said to receive either water baptism or the Spirit through Priscilla and Aquila, and it is highly unlikely that Luke would fail to mention Apollos's Spirit Baptism; (2) Apollos is well versed in Scripture; (3) Apollos had been instructed in the way of the Lord; (4) Apollos taught accurately the things concerning Jesus; (5) Apollos is said to be "boiling over in the Spirit."

In view of the fact that in Acts $\pi\nu\epsilon\hat{\upsilon}\mu\alpha$ connotes the human spirit only twice, and in both cases personal pronouns are attached making this evident (7:59, 17:16), it is very likely that this term refers to the Holy Spirit. Is it the human spirit that impels one to teach correctly the things concerning Jesus? Point three shows that it was not only the earthly Jesus or the Jesus prophesied in the Old Testament that Apollos knew of, but also "the way of the Lord."

In all likelihood Apollos simply need to be instructed about water baptism and to be baptized, similar to other cases of those who had received the Spirit but not water baptism (Cornelius, for instance). If we ask how it is that Apollos became converted without receiving water baptism, we can only give a conjecture for an answer. One may suggest that Apollos, knowing his Old Testament, had heard Christians preaching in the synagogue—a preaching that did not involve a call to water baptism. Perhaps, upon reflection after the meeting, he was convicted, converted, and then received the Spirit.

This text may also imply that Apollos was not attached to any Christian community in particular where he could be baptized, and he might have gone immediately on the road after his conversion to share his new faith with fellow Jews in the synagogues. In any case, Priscilla and Aquila either heard him say or fail to say something about the Christian initiation/conversion process, and they then instructed him "more accurately" and may even have baptized him. Though Luke does not mention Apollos's baptism, it has been suggested that the Ephesian Christians would not have recommended him to Corinth if he had not been baptized (cf. Acts 18:27). It is interesting to speculate about the possibility that once Apollos received correct teaching about Christian baptism, he emphasized this when he went to Corinth. If so, then perhaps those who say, "I am of Apollos" (1 Cor 1:12, 14-17) are those who received water baptism from Apollos. Is Paul distinguishing himself from Apollos in his baptizing and eloquent wisdom in 1 Corinthians 1:17? Perhaps.

Thus, Acts 18 does teach us that a person can be truly Christian without water baptism. This is not to say that the rite is optional, but its necessity is not because it is necessary for salvation, but because it is necessary to obey Jesus in His command (Matthew 28:19-20). The conjecture of Beasley-Murray that John's baptism was sufficient for

Apollos since he had the Spirit seems most unlikely, especially in view of what immediately follows in Acts 19:1-4.[21]

In Acts 19:1-7, we have disciples (a term used elsewhere in Acts exclusively of Christians) of John who have received neither Christian water nor Spirit Baptism. Paul obviously knew something was wrong when he spoke with them, for though they evidenced some sort of faith, Paul felt led to ask, "Did you receive the Spirit when you believed?" It is clear from this initial question what was crucial in Paul's (and/or Luke's) eyes: not faith or a water rite, but the Spirit. Note, however, that Paul did not fail to water baptize them in his concern for the central fact that made one a Christian. John's water baptism was no substitute or equivalent to Christian water baptism. Their reply seems quite astounding at first. How could a disciple of John the Baptizer, who preached about the coming Spirit Baptism, claim they had never heard of the Holy Spirit?

The answer is probably to be sought in the fact that "there must have been many people who had some contact with John or Jesus only at a certain point in their ministries. . . . For example, there would be those who knew only the repentance baptism of John; those who knew and believed in no more than John's teaching; those who knew Jesus only in the flesh."[22] When we add the fact that those who lived outside of the Holy Land received such teaching second- or third-hand, it is understandable that there would be those who had not heard of the existence of the Holy Spirit.

When the disciples answered Paul's question, the apostle knew he had to start the initiation process from step one. Thus, it seems likely that we have in Acts 19:4-6 Paul's (and Luke's) idea of what would be the normal order of initiation into the covenant community for someone entering from the outside: water baptism then Spirit Baptism. Paul describes John's baptism as one of repentance, a preparation for the One who came after John (that is, Jesus). Unfortunately, he does not tell us what sort of baptism the Christian rite is, though we are told it involves baptism in the name of the Lord Jesus. We are not told, however, if it involves profession of faith, but presumably they inducted those desiring to be baptized on their willingness to accept Jesus.

Further, no mention is made of repentance, and perhaps Paul (or Luke) means to distinguish the Christian rite from John's in this respect—by describing the distinctive feature of John's baptism as one of repentance and preparation, while saying that the Christian rite is done in the name of the Lord Jesus. Here we see a complete initiation where the conversion process takes place in a very short space of time. The interval between water and Spirit (as well as of laying on hands attached to the latter) distinguishes the two, but the shortness of the interval reveals that they are closely related. I have reversed Dunn's term (conversion-initiation) because it appears now that the normal order is water then Spirit and that, while water is an initiatory rite, the reception of the Spirit by faith is the conversion. Further, it appears that, all things being equal, the two baptisms should come in close proximity, at least in the case of proselytes entering from outside the believing community, so that sign and thing signified can be linked in a meaningful way. There surely is no justification here for speaking of a two-stage process of believing and then later being baptized in the Spirit "to empower for ministry."[23] Having seen Luke portraying Paul as normally proceeding in the order of initiation then Spirit reception, let us see how it actually happened to Paul. As is well known, three accounts appear in Acts of this celebrated Damascus road incident.

PAUL'S CONVERSION AND BAPTISM

In the minds of many Christians, when someone says, "Damascus road," the immediate response is "the conversion of Paul." While this association is partly correct, it is better to speak not of a crisis event, but of a crisis experience extending over the three days from the Damascus road to his baptism.[24] Paul's blindness for three days, his commissioning which he received through the vision and through Ananias, and his exhortation by Ananias in 22:16 all point to the fact that we are dealing with a process of enlightenment and change, not an instant conversion and commissioning at Damascus with Spirit Baptism and/ or water baptism added on three days later.

Only two of the accounts concern us: Acts 9 and Acts 22. Perhaps it will help to lay out what Ananias and Paul did, so that we can understand the relation of water and Spirit in these narratives. Paul had seen the risen Lord—a sight that blinded him temporarily but which illuminated his thoughts and letters from then on (cf. Gal 1:1, 15; 1 Cor 15:8).

Perhaps we may expect that the other parts of his conversion experience—his water baptism and Spirit Baptism—affected him as much. In Acts 9:17, Ananias's role is (1) to heal Paul by laying on of hands, and (2) to lay hands on Paul so that he may be filled with the Spirit. In Acts 9:18, we are told that Paul (1) received his sight again, got up, and (2) was baptized (water or Spirit?). In Acts 22:13, 16, Ananias's role is (1) to give Paul his sight (22:13); and (2) to exhort Paul to arise and be baptized, washing away his sins, and calling on Jesus' name. If we only had Acts 9.17-18, one might conclude that the reference to baptism in Acts 9.18 refers to Spirit baptism. If we only had Acts 22.13-16, we would assume that Paul received water baptism, since washing away of sins is mentioned.

Elsewhere in Acts, however, only the Spirit can make a person spiritually clean (cf. Acts 10:15, 28, 44-47, the point of verse 47 is that, if they have been cleansed through the Spirit by God, then surely they cannot be refused water baptism, which symbolizes this cleansing). To confuse the issue further, we may note that in Acts 15:8-9, the giving of the Spirit is nearly synonymous with God "purifying their hearts through faith." What we have in 15:8-9, as we often find in Paul's letters, is the use of water baptism language to describe Spirit baptism.

For Paul, water baptism and Spirit Baptism possibly took place simultaneously, though they are not synonymous, and this may explain why there are difficulties in deciding which is which in his letters. Alternatively, we may argue that Paul received sight and the Spirit simultaneously, in reaction to which Paul got up and received water baptism.

Elsewhere in Acts (chaps. 8 and 19) receiving the Spirit is associated with the laying on of hands, so this may point to Paul receiving the Spirit before water baptism. This is all the more likely if Paul's blindness also symbolizes spiritual blindness,[25] and his recovery of physical sight was the external and visible sign of his gaining the Spirit and spiritual sight. Perhaps no mention is made of Paul's water baptism (as with Apollos), but is it conceivable that Luke would omit Paul's Spirit Baptism?

In Acts 10:43, Peter speaks of receiving the forgiveness of sins, and Cornelius receives the Spirit, implying again that any real washing of a person is through God's Spirit.[26] Though the issue is complicated, I lean toward the view that Paul received Spirit Baptism with physical sight and then water baptism. If this is so, then in Acts 22:16 we are told that water baptism represents a washing away of sin that Spirit Baptism accomplishes. We are also told, however, that involved in water baptism is a calling on Jesus' name. The main verbs in the sentence are *to wash* and *to be baptized*, and the *calling* is a subordinate participial phrase qualifying either one or both these verbs. It may refer to an actual act by the baptized while he is being "washed." This is perhaps most likely in this case. It seems possible that the calling on the name of the Lord refers to what in fact the act of baptism and washing symbolizes: an appeal to God. This last suggestion may be given weight by examining 9:14, where Paul is said to be coming to arrest all those who call upon Jesus' name—that is, all Christians and perhaps all the baptized. Whether water baptism is an appeal, or whether it is associated with an appeal or an invoking of the name (in part a confession, but more an appeal for salvation from the "name"), we have here evidence that water baptism is not the thing in itself. As Barth said of the baptismal formula, it is likewise true of the act itself—it is teleological. It points to something other than itself. If received in the order water then Spirit, then it is a preparatory act that points forward to Spirit Baptism. If received in the reverse order, then there is still the element of appeal to God for the washing away of sins and thus for future salvation in the divine "name." As in the case of Jesus, who prayed after water baptism and before Spirit Baptism, so here an appeal is involved with and/or in water baptism. Bear this in mind as we examine the material in the Pauline letters and 1 Peter.

To sum up what we have learned here about initiation-conversion, we must first consider when the process of conversion begins. Does it begin before we are willing or ready for it to happen, much less ready to confess it? The example of Paul is the classic case. While his conversion frequently has been assumed to be instantaneous, in fact it was not. As Dunn rightly says, "I do not deny that Paul's whole Weltanschauung changed as a result of the single incident on the Damascus road: I do deny that it changed in a single moment."[27] The process of Paul's conversion took three days and began with an act of God that (1) did not presuppose Paul's confession, (2) did not presuppose Paul's conversion or faith, and (3) accosted Paul with the fact that he was against such a confession of faith. In short, God made Paul an offer he could not refuse. If a gracious God may begin the process of initiation which ends in conversion, can the church, who are God's emissaries and who have been given the authority to forgive sins (cf. John 20:23; Matt 16:19, 18:18) likewise begin the initiation process for an individual before he can or will respond?

If it is argued that the church must wait for a candidate to do his part and repent and confess his sins, one will do well to remember that while repentance is our act, it is also something God grants an individual (Acts 11:18). It also may be argued that for God to initiate the process of conversion as only God can do is one thing; it is quite another for the church to begin the process of initiation that may or may not end in conversion. This point is well taken, but I also remind those who argue in this way that initiation, like conversion, is a process, not an act, for it involves two baptisms, not one.

Furthermore, on the basis of Acts, I see no grounds for the view that a confession of faith is a prerequisite for baptism. Repentance appears to be such a prerequisite, in some cases, and willingness to submit to water baptism as well; however, there is no stress in Acts on the necessity of a confession prior to water baptism. In the one case where apparently there was evidence of belief or sincerity prior to water baptism, things went very wrong (Acts 8). True enough, an abuse does not argue against a proper use, but still we must ask whether or not we can say that confession of faith is the necessary prerequisite to water baptism.

The Western text of the Ethiopian eunuch story thought so, but that is not a part of our canon. Even in the most celebrated conversion story in Acts, we do not have recorded a confession of faith prior to water baptism, but at most an invocation or appeal with or through water baptism. I am not trying to minimize the importance of a good profession of faith. I am questioning, however, the assumption that we may deduce from Acts that a profession of faith is necessary as a prerequisite to water baptism.

In Acts we have seen more than one pattern of initiation-conversion: water then Spirit; Spirit then water; and perhaps in Paul's or the twelve Ephesians' case, water and Spirit almost simultaneously. I incline to the view that the first is the more normal pattern, though I refrain from calling it normative since there is strong attestation in Acts for its converse. Regardless, these texts give no justification for an interval between the two baptisms, especially if Spirit Baptism comes first. It appears that water baptism is revealed in Acts to be a preparatory and symbolic rite. Acts 8 especially shows that water baptism is anything but *ex opere operato*, and the story of Apollos shows us that it is not necessary for conversion or salvation. As we have seen in Acts 22, water baptism is associated with the cleansing that God's Spirit performs. We have noted also the household principle of inclusion in the community, but argued that there was no evidence for infant baptism in these texts. Such household inclusions may be more a result of God's grace than of the missionary principles or factors exhibited in Acts.

We have argued strongly for the fact that baptism in the Spirit is the sine qua non, the thing without which one is not a Christian. This fact in itself, coupled with the narrative in Acts 2:38ff. and Acts 19, intimates that water baptism is intended to be a preparatory initiation rite. As such, both the act of water baptism and its language and preaching (particularly in Acts 2:38) are dependent on and reminiscent of John's baptism. Acts 19 shows, however, clear differences. Christian baptism is in Jesus' name and bears witness to the salvation history events of death, resurrection, and Spirit giving that happened to and through him. John's baptism is no satisfactory substitute for the true Christian rite in view of the accomplished work of Jesus, which is the foundation and background to the Christian water rite. In view of this, Christian water baptism is not only a preparatory rite in what it symbolizes (the negative side of conversion, that is, cleansing, putting off the old nature), but also in what it signifies about its recipient (that is, the initiation-conversion process has begun).

Chapter 4

TRIAL BY WATER ORDEAL

Paul and Burial with Christ

DOES BAPTISM SAVE, IN PAUL'S VIEW?

Any study of Paul's view of baptism is advised to start by remembering what we have already noted—that 1 Corinthains 1 says clearly and succinctly that Paul is glad he did not baptize more Corinthians, but we surely cannot imagine him ever saying "I thank God I did not convert more Corinthians." Nor, at the end of 1 Corinthians (15:29) should we miss the fact that while Paul does not endorse the Corinthian practice of "baptism for the dead," he also does not pause to correct this practice either. Clearly, baptism is not at the top of Paul's list of things to teach or worry about. And surely 1 Corinthians 1 rules out an overly sacramental approach to Paul's view of water baptism.

But even more to the point let us consider for a minute 1 Corinthians 10:1-12. Paul draws a creative analogy between the "Old Testament sacraments" that the Israelites shared in, and the "New Testament sacraments" the Corinthians are sharing in. The major point he wishes to make is that just as those gracious acts of God in the Old Testament did not in themselves save the participants, so also the Corinthians need to avoid some sort of magical view of baptism, as if it saved persons and in some sense sealed them for eternity, even if they sinned with impunity. His point is surely that such rituals without a godly life are no guarantee of salvation or even present spiritual well-being. Of course the analogy between baptism and the Red Sea crossing is inexact to say the least. The Israelites walked across on dry land, and one would be hard pressed to even conclude that the analogy favors the notion of sprinkling, so little contact did the Israelites have with the water. After all Pharaoh's army got totally immersed, indeed drowned in the water. There was indeed a trial by water ordeal, but not, alas, a saving one.

We need to be able to make critical distinctions between when Paul is using the powerful water baptismal language to talk about something else—namely conversion or the beginnings of Christian experience—and when he is actually discussing the subject of water baptism itself. Furthermore, we need to be exceedingly cautious about overreading texts that may be talking about the event of passage from darkness to light, using the language of the rite of passage, when in fact Paul is really talking about spiritual experience, not what happens to a person because of the rite of water baptism itself. Look, for example, at Galatians 3:27-28. Here, one might think, we have a clear example where faith, the act of water baptism, spiritual transformation, and perhaps even a catechetical formula are all working hand in glove to tell us what happens when a person is baptized.

One can look at Beasley-Murray's work and immediately discover a line of thinking which suggests that Paul has an elaborated theology of what water baptism can and does accomplish, at least if one approaches it in faith.[1] The problem with such a conclusion is that Paul has already decisively distinguished water baptism from conversion in 1 Corinthians 1. There were many converts. By no means were all of them baptized by Paul when he was with them. Some became Christians quite apart from the rite of water baptism. Indeed, so disgusted is Paul with the overly magical or overly sacramental view of baptism that some in his audience have that he throws up his hands in disgust and says, "thank heavens I didn't baptize more of you." This fact must be uppermost in one's mind when one reads what Paul says in texts like Galatians 3:27-28.

Notice in the first place that we do not have the noun *baptism* here in Galatians 3:27. What we have instead is the verbal phrase *was baptized into Christ*. Paul has just said, in the immediately preceding sentence, that "all are sons of God through faith in Christ Jesus." That seems clear enough. The means by which one becomes a son or daughter of God is through faith in Christ. What then should we make of the next phrase, "for whoever was baptized into Christ has 'put on/clothed themselves' with Christ"? There can be no doubt that the language here is influenced by what happened in the baptismal ritual. One took off one's clothing (or at least some of it), one was baptized, and then one put on clothing again, perhaps new clothing symbolizing one's new state of being. But it must be stressed that when Paul says that a person "has clothed themselves with Christ," he is not talking about the ritual itself.

How do we know? We must consider 1 Corinthians 12:13, where Paul is crystal clear about what he means. The verse reads as follows: "But we have all been baptized into Christ's body by one Spirit and we were all given one Spirit to drink." Immediately apparent is that the language is highly metaphorical. One does not literally drink in the Holy Spirit. But notice who Paul says is the one who baptized a person into Christ's body—the Holy Spirit himself! Paul is discussing in 1 Corinthians 12 the Holy Spirit and spiritual gifts. Water baptism is nowhere the subject of discussion, and Paul has chosen to describe the spiritual experience of conversion by using the highly symbolic and metaphorical language, including baptismal language. In short, when Paul wants to talk about the actual spiritual transaction, he talks about faith and the work of the Holy Spirit on and in the person. The confusion is entirely ours because he uses baptismal language to convey the richness of his meaning. One more thing: notice the word *all* in 1 Corinthians 12:13 "we all were baptized" says Paul here, which contrasts with the clear statement in 1 Corinthians 1 that Paul had not water baptized all those who were saved in Corinth. This is no problem since

Paul is talking only about water baptism in 1 Corinthians 1, but he is only discussing Spirit Baptism in 1 Corinthians 12.

So let us return now to Galatians 3:27-28. Is Paul really saying that if you get yourself water baptized you will have this benefit of becoming sons of God or being saved? Or should we rather note that here in Galatians 3.27 we have exactly the same verb *was baptized*, as in 1 Corinthians 12:13 (here in third singular; in 1 Cor 12:13 in the first plural). Notice no mention is made at all in either text of a human agent of baptism. I must then conclude that Paul in both texts is referring to the work of the Holy Spirit which grafts a person "into Christ," by which is meant "into Christ's body." This is the same thing as saying a person has "clothed themselves with Christ." What we may deduce is that salvation is by the gracious work of the Spirit, but it is through active faith appropriation, hence the aorist middle verb "has clothed oneself." I am afraid that while we can learn a great deal about Paul's theology of conversion here, we cannot learn too much about his theological of ritual initiation. But, some will say, a text is available that much more clearly expounds Paul's view of water baptism: Romans 6:1-4, to which we now turn.

BURIAL WITH CHRIST IN BAPTISM: TRIAL BY WATER ORDEAL

The ritual of trial by water ordeal is an ancient one, going back at least to the Code of Hammurabi, and even earlier. It took various forms, and may in fact be related to the trial by bitter waters we find in Numbers 5. In 1 Corinthians 10, which we have already mentioned above, Paul depicts the Red Sea crossing as a trial by water ordeal, with some being redeemed (the Israelites) and some being judged (the Egyptians). That Paul uses the language of being "baptized into Moses" to describe this salvation historical event is telling. He sees a clear analogy between that event and water baptism. We may wish to also compare Joshua 4-5 where we have another passing through the waters (on dry land!), this time into the promised land.[2]

When we are dealing with Paul's theology of water baptism, several facts must be kept in view:

(1) he was a highly trained Pharisee who knew the Torah intimately and also, of course, Jewish traditions about water rites and rituals;

(2) we have no evidence that Paul derives his theology of baptism from some teaching of Jesus, or even the early church. There is this similarity between what we find in Paul and Acts– baptism is said to be into Christ in the Pauline corpus, and in Acts it is done in the name of Jesus;

(3) we may suspect that Paul knew about John the Baptizer and his water ritual in the Jordan, though he never mentions it. What he would have learned about John would presumably include that John connected his water rite with the coming judgment of Yahweh, as a way of preparing for and averting the "wrath to come."

That is, John presented his water ritual that involved repentance in the face of coming judgment as a sort of water ordeal. Bearing this in mind, let's look closely at Romans 6, and especially at its odd language about being buried with Christ in baptism. We need to keep in mind a few questions: Is the covenant sign of the New Covenant like the covenant sign of the Mosaic Covenant? In other words, what aspect of the covenant does it symbolize? Does it symbolize what is being left behind (and a promise not to return to it), or what is yet to come? In short, in Paul's theology is it a sign of the oath curse sanction, or the promised blessing?

In the first place, Paul's major subject in Romans 6:1-14 is not baptism but rather sin, death, law versus grace, life and a related constellation of ideas. Furthermore, as was the case in 1 Corinthians 12 and Galatians 3, Paul says nothing about the humans who administer the rite of baptism here. His real concern is with the spiritual experience shadowed forth in the ritual, which is why even so conservative a commentator as Douglas Moo says, "[W]e must assume from the fact that faith is emblazoned in every chapter of Romans while baptism is mentioned in only two verses that genuine faith, even if it has not been 'sealed' in baptism, is sufficient for salvation."[3] This is precisely what one would deduce from 1 Corinthians as well.

Here Paul explains that being baptized into Christ amounts to being baptized into his death. Put another way, he says it's all about the fact that "we were buried with him through baptism into death." In the previous sentence he spoke of "having died to sin." At first this all sounds rather grim. Baptism is associated with death and burial, in particular death to sin, and this is somehow spiritually connected to Jesus' own death on the cross, such that to be baptized into Christ means to be baptized into his death, which somehow entails or produces our own death to sin. In verse 4 death is not seen here so much as an event as a state into which we enter. Notice that throughout this discussion baptism is not associated with or seen to depict resurrection, but rather what comes before resurrection: death and burial. Resurrection is rather paralleled with the subsequent walking in newness of life, something that comes after the spiritual death of the old person.

Here it is germane to point to a text like 2 Corinthians 5:17 and compare it to Romans 6:6. Paul actually believes that the old self, the old person has died, has been crucified with Christ, is dead and buried, and that this is what water baptism symbolizes: the death and burial of the old person—in other words, the negative side of conversion, referring to what has been left behind.[4] This brings us back to those questions we raised briefly before.

Circumcision was clearly enough the sign of the oath curse of the Mosaic covenant, of the threat that God would "cut off" a person who did not keep the covenant signed by the ritual act. Paul elsewhere suggests that Christ's death is a sort of circumcision, a sort of enacting of the oath curse of God on Jesus, in our stead. Consider what Colossians 2:11-12 says "in him you were also circumcised with a circumcision not performed by human hands, in the putting off of the body of flesh, in the circumcision of Christ having been buried with him in baptism." Here at the end of the phrase we have a virtually identical remark to what was said in Romans 6, with one difference. Paul in Colossians refers to Christ's death elliptically as "the circumcision of Christ." He had earlier said in Colossians 1 that God had reconciled us to himself through the very body (and death) of Jesus. How then do we put these pieces together and make sense of Paul's theology of baptism?

First there is the Christ event. Christ's death is the enactment of the oath curse on Christ himself, which is called "the circumcision of Christ." Second, Paul then says that when we are converted to Christ, our own old natures are cut off and put to death, which in effect is a circumcision in us. Third, he makes clear that he is not talking about the effect of the ritual in Colossians 2:11-12, for he says this transpires through a circumcision not done by human hands. Fourth, he draws an analogy between the putting off of the flesh, the old nature, and the having been buried with Christ in baptism, the subject already discussed in Romans 6. What seems clear enough is that Paul has deliberately drawn a parallel between baptism and circumcision, suggesting that baptism in his mind depicts the enactment of the oath curse as well—only in this case, the symbolism of judgment is of being "overwhelmed" in the flood, and so drowning, dying, and (just to mix the metaphors), being buried (at sea). This is one way to talk about the ancient water ordeal. But how then should we make sense of all this archaic language?

First of all, what baptism depicts is what we sometimes call regeneration. It depicts the work of God in the life of the person, such that the old sinful nature dies. Baptism does not depict our faith response to that work of God, but rather what precedes and enables it: the divine work, which brings us back to a crucial point. Baptism is a passive sacrament or symbol—something done only once—and as such depicts a rite of passage into Christ's community. It is something done on behalf of the participant. One does not baptize oneself. In other words, the pure symbolism of baptism in Paul, like the spiritual transformation it depicts, is not synergistic, nor does it presuppose the faith response. Now, of course, in Romans 6 and in Colossians 2 Paul is thinking of missionary baptisms in which initiation, regeneration, conversion, and faith response all come together in a short span of time as someone enters the covenant community from outside that community. In none of these texts is Paul in fact dealing with the second-order or second-generation question of what to do with infants or small children of believers. He is thinking of missionary baptisms.

What can we deduce from the language used about burial in regard to the mode of baptism? The word βαπτίζειν itself means something like being "overwhelmed," and clearly enough immersion would be a more apt picture of burial than, say sprinkling or pouring would be. But however apt, no mode of baptism is prescribed by Paul anywhere. And the word *baptize* itself need not be translated as "immerse," though it certainly can refer to immersion. Jewish rituals of cleansing, while they could involve immersing one's self, could also involve something less dramatic, like simple washing without going under the water entirely. It is not even clear in the case of John the baptizer that everyone was being immersed, though if he was at a spot in the Jordan where there was enough water (which was not always the case), immersion could have been practiced. This brings us back to the trial by water ordeal.

One form that the trial by water ordeal took is that a stone was tied to a person and he was put in a body of water. If he sank, he was guilty; if he floated, he was innocent. Jesus may be referring to this very ordeal when he talks about it being better to tie a millstone around one's neck and be thrown into the sea than if one causes a little one to stumble (Matt 18:6). I am suggesting then that Paul has this constellation of ideas in mind when he thinks of baptism: (1) It is a covenant sign, like circumcision, and it depicts the same sort of thing—judgment on sin; (2) Paul associates baptism with the death and burial of Jesus, and is even prepared to call Jesus' death his circumcision; (3) baptism dramatically depicts the death of the old person, his death to sin, by being grafted into the death and burial of Jesus.

Rising to newness of life, walking into life, and the like are the sequel to this conversion or regeneration event, but those things are not depicted in baptism. This is understandable since baptism depicts the cleansing out or off of the old dirt, the old self, the old sin. All of this discussion comports quite nicely with what Dunn has to say when he stresses that one has to be able to distinguish in these texts between the spiritual experience and the symbolic depiction of that experience in baptism.[5] What then should we conclude from this discussion?

AND SO?

The primary significance of water baptism for Paul lies in what it symbolizes and the fact that it is a valid picture, a visible word proclaiming and depicting Christ's death and God's judgment on sin, our burial with Christ, and God's provision for us not through water baptism itself, but through the greater baptism of the Spirit. The Spirit immerses and grafts one into Christ, not any human being or any human ritual wrought by human hands. Paul does not associate baptism with resurrection, but rather with death and burial, and thus is not drawing on the Hellenistic or mystery religion notions about dying and rising through the ritual. For Paul, what water baptism symbolizes is close to what circumcision meant, and from Colossians 2 it is hard not to believe that Paul saw water baptism as in one sense the Christian's circumcision. Probably he saw baptism as a rite of passage similar to, but replacing, circumcision, which was the sign of an earlier, and now defunct, covenant.

Baptism symbolizes and looks back to Christ's death, and depicts the believer's death to sin, the termination of the old fallen self, and indeed its burial once and for all. It also foreshadows or depicts Spirit Baptism, the actual act that produces what water baptism only depicts. More often than not for Paul, baptism, being such a powerful and rich symbol, shaped his vocabulary when he wanted to talk about regeneration or conversion. Water baptism was clearly a ritual he did and was prepared to perform, but he had a considerable concern that his converts not read too much into the ritual itself (1 Cor 1). In a sense, one could say water baptism was a sign, an oath sign, and thus more than an ordinary symbol. It was a visible word of God depicting God's judgment on sin, and indeed his desire to renew and redeem and regenerate even the sinner. So far as we can see, Paul does not view water baptism itself as a means of grace. That transpires by the work of the Holy Spirit. Nor is there evidence that Paul saw water baptism as a seal of preexisting Christian faith. In following him we would do well not to overestimate or overtheologize water baptism and thereby have the unfortunate effect of diminishing the importance of the marvelous and miraculous thing that it symbolizes: cleansing from sin, washing away of the old self, the death and burial of the old nature and the like.

Wayne Meeks in his helpful study on Paul and his communities has this to say about how baptism likely was practiced in the Pauline churches:

> The center of the ritual, as the terms βαπτίζειν and βάπτισμα indicate, was simply a water bath. In one of Paul's reminders, the conversion of Corinthians from their former life of vice is summarized thus: "But you were washed, you were made holy, you were justified in [or by] the name of our Lord Jesus Christ and in [or by] the Spirit of our God" (1 Cor. 6.11). The fact that baptism could be construed as a symbolic burial with Christ (Rom. 6.4; Col. 2.12) suggests a complete immersion in water. That was the case with the normal rite of purification, the tebilah, which was probably, at whatever distance, the primary antecedent of Christian baptism. The first full description of the Christian rite, in Hippolytus' Apostolic Tradition, which probably represents Roman practice at the end of the second century, attests a threefold immersion. However, the little manual of church order called the Didache ("Teaching of the Twelve Apostles"), which may represent traditions as much as a century older than Hippolytus, probably in Syria, provides for pouring water thrice over the head, in case sufficient water for immersion is not at hand (7.3).[6]

These remarks are helpful, in allowing us to see Paul's practice both in light of the Jewish background and the Christian foreground. Note, though, that while it is mentioned in passing in the little credo statement in Ephesians 4:5, water baptism was to become a part of the faith confessed. It was to be "one," like the one true faith, and like the one true Lord. Unlike Jewish ritual cleansing, baptism was not to be a repeated ritual.

We should ask, in light of the clearly Jewish background, why not? Why was baptism only to be "one" performed on a person only once? Why not repeatedly? Why not annually? Why not practice rebaptism?

The answer seems to be simple. This ritual did not depict the repeated renewal of faith that is necessary in a repeated confession of faith. It depicted the one-time rite of passage from being the old person to being the new person. Ideally, it should be performed as closely in time to Spirit Baptism as is possible. But sometimes, as Acts shows, water baptism would be practiced before Spirit Baptism, and sometimes afterwards, and sometimes almost with a harmonic convergence of the sign and the thing signified. But by definition one only crosses the line once into the covenant community for the first time, just as one can only step into the river for the first time once. Water baptism is about first things. It is about the regenerating action of God that results in the death and burial of the old self, the old sin, the old "flesh." That transition, that rite of passage was supposed to happen but once in a person's life. Again Meeks helps us when he writes, "By making the cleansing rite alone bear the whole function of initiation, and by making initiation the decisive point of entry into an exclusive community, the Christian groups create something new. For them, the bath becomes a permanent threshold between the 'clean' group and the 'dirty' world, between those who have been initiated and everyone who has not."[7] As such, washing as the initiatory rite would normally precede the filling of the now holy vessel with God's Spirit. Water baptism is a matter of a plea to "create in me a clean heart O God" and "renew a right spirit within me."

Thus, overreading texts like Romans 6:3-4 and Colossians 2:11-12, as Beasley-Murray does, is just as unhelpful as trivializing or ignoring such texts.[8] Did you notice that the first verb in 1 Corinthians 6:11 is not "but you were justified" but rather "you were washed" and then "you were set apart" or "made holy"? Justification is only mentioned third in this sequence of verbs. I submit that this is no accident. As Meeks goes on to say, washing was often preparatory for initiation. One had to be clean before one could be initiated.

For Paul, water baptism is doubtless an initiatory rite, not a confirmation ritual, which helps explain how it was even possible for Philip to baptize Samaritans before they demonstrated the presence of the Holy Spirit in their lives. He was simply initiating them into the new covenant community. They did not receive the Spirit by this ritual. These two baptisms can and should be distinguished.[9] One is a boundary marker; the other actually enacts what the rite only depicts. Nowhere is this clearer than in Galatians 3:27-28, where we are told that in Christ there is no Jew or Gentile, no slave or free, no male and female, but all are one in Christ. This sort of remarkable change would require a miraculous spiritual transformation that no rite could ever produce. Bearing this in mind, we now consider the Johannine literature.

Chapter 5

BREAKING THE WATERS OF BIRTH

Water Baptism in the Johannine Literature?

An unusual fact about Beasley-Murray's book on baptism is the about-face he does when he gets to the Johannine literature. After finding references to water baptism virtually everywhere that water, cleansing, or confession is mentioned in Paul, he finds references virtually nowhere in John, which is often called the sacramental gospel. I suspect that his approach is a reaction to Cullmann's work on baptism and on the sacramental allusions in John: Cullmann does to John what Beasley-Murray does to Paul. I am skeptical of the efforts of Cullmann and Beasley-Murray for two reasons: (1) the Fourth Evangelist, like Paul, uses sacramental language to discuss something other than the sacraments, and (2) what is often assumed to be the Fourth Evangelist's sacramentalism is more likely his attempts to emphasize the physical reality of the Word made flesh in order to combat any docetic tendencies. The Fourth Evangelist uses sacramental language to express his incarnational theology, not the reverse.

THE WATERS OF BIRTH: JOHN 3:5

In order to appreciate the use of water language in this gospel, one needs to read the following texts: 1:26, 31, 33, 2:1-11, 3:5, 3:22-26, 4:7-15, (4:46), 5:2-9, 7:37-39, 9:7, 11, 13:1-16, and 19:34. In these verses, one notes that our author uses water in two different ways: (1) as an example of the old dispensation in its preparedness or lack of efficacy, and (2) in contrasting fashion, as a symbol of the new dispensation, the spiritual, which comes from above. As Dunn rightly says, the water references in chapters 1, 2, 3, and 5, with the possible exception of 3:5, represent that which is part of the old dispensation. In chapters 4, 7, and 19, however, water is a metaphor of the Spirit.[1] Dunn thus admits that water, in the immediate context of the Nicodemus story, is used to represent the old dispensation.

In John 3:22ff., for instance, we have the familiar episode referring to John's water baptism and its preparatory nature for the One who was already taking away some of John's following. In John 2:1ff., we have the story of the water changed to wine, where the water represents the old dispensation with its lack of life and verve, its inability to give cause for celebration or rejoicing. Set in this context, we would expect water in John 3:5 to represent something that has to do with the old order, not with Christian water baptism. For this reason Dunn suggests that water in John 3:5 refers to John's baptism, but even he is not satisfied with this idea.[2]

I think one key to the story in chapter 3 is found in verse 12: "I have spoken to you of earthly things and you do not believe; how then will you believe if I speak of heavenly things?" Jesus tentatively suggests the subject of being born again or born from above,[3] and begins to introduce the new thing amidst the old. Thus, here is the way the passage should be understood: Jesus says that you must be born again, which might (but apparently does not) conjure up to Nicodemus images of being a proselyte. Nicodemus thinks that Jesus is referring to a second physical birth; thus, he says, "How can a man be born when he is old? Surely he cannot enter a second time into his womb to be born!" Jesus replies, "Truly, unless a man is born of flesh (i.e., physically) and Spirit, he cannot enter the Kingdom of God. Flesh gives birth to flesh, but Spirit gives birth to Spirit. You should not be surprised at my saying, 'You must be born again.'" Interpreting water as physical birth is not without precedent in ancient literature.[4] The birth process itself shows that water can be an appropriate symbol for such an event, for example, when the "water" breaks, it is one of the first signs that the child is coming forth. As birth was a common occurrence in the homes in Jesus' day, such an allusion would not be lost on Jesus' or John's audience. John's contact with the intimate details of Palestinian life have been noted in other contexts. In fact, the grammar of this particular verse supports such a conclusion, for the Greek reads literally "born out of water." Second, such a use of the water language in this way makes sense in this context. It is natural that Jesus should begin where Nicodemus leaves off—in the mother's womb (4b)—when he starts his reply. Further, verse 6 confirms this view, for it clearly says what was said in verse 5b, but in a slightly different fashion. Also, the use of water in this way comports with its association with the old dispensation, the things that are from "below," from this physical existence. What better way to prepare his readers for an analogous use of water in the new dispensation referring to spiritual rebirth and renewal than to use it of physical birth in the old dispensation?

Finally, nothing could make more sense in the context of Johannine theology and in the original setting of this story in the life of Jesus. As we have said, the Fourth Evangelist is not so much on a campaign against antisacramentalists as he is fighting docetic tendencies by his incarnational theology. To insist not only that Jesus had a physical birth and nature, but also that we too must have the same as a prerequisite to spiritual rebirth, might seem obvious to us, but there were people in the evangelist's time who wished to downplay or downgrade our physical natures as somewhat less than good. John, by contrast, wishes to emphasize intimate connection of the physical and the spiritual in us, as in Christ. This close linking of physical and spirit is evidence here in the phrase *water and Spirit*, which are both the object of only one preposition: ἐκ which means "out of." The point is that the physical or old dispensation is not bad; in fact, it is the necessary prerequisite to spiritual rebirth. Grace presupposes and transforms nature, but the physical order is not sufficient in itself for salvation and real life. The water is not bad because it is water (John 2), but it was better when transformed into wine. The Fourth Evangelist is trying to maintain a careful balance. The new thing—Spirit, spiritual rebirth, new life—is what the gospel is about. This evangelist, however, wishes also to remind us that this new development should not cause us to devalue the old physical order. In fact, the ultimate endorsement of the new came from God, who not only created it, but reaffirmed its essential goodness when "the Word became flesh and lived for a while among us" (1:44).

But what of the significance of John 3:5 in its original setting? Jesus would not refer the Christian rite of baptism to Nicodemus, but he certainly might speak of physical and spiritual births. The evangelist does not seem to be in the business of inserting references to the sacraments in his gospel. The most that can be said is that he used sacramental language to describe the events and realities of salvation history. The author of this gospel knew that inserting a reference, not just an allusion, to Christian baptism or its language in the midst of the Nicodemus story is not only bad history, but also bad story-telling. Rather, I believe that the Fourth Evangelist might use traditional, even sacramental, language as he wrote of the eternal verities. If, as I think unlikely, there is an allusion to water baptism, then such an allusion serves here to point away from itself to the realities it depicts. One should not say more. Since at most we have the language of water baptism used to speak of something other than the rite itself, we can probably learn nothing here of a proper order of baptism, though it is interesting that the order is water then Spirit. Finally, there is absolutely no reason for seeing in this passage the idea that water baptism is necessary for salvation.[5]

JOHN 19:34: BLOOD OR WATER–WHICH IS THICKER?

The story of Jesus' death is rich in symbolism of various sorts. But seeing an allusion to either baptism or the Eucharist in the story of the spear that pierced Jesus' side, prompting blood and water to come forth, is unlikely.

The problems with seeing any reference to water baptism are as follows:

(1) blood is mentioned first, and the Lord's Supper was not ever the initial or initiatory rite. Furthermore, blood alone is never the symbol for the Lord's Supper;

(2) there probably is a connection here to John 7:38, which is speaking of "living water" in the believer and refers to the new life that we have through the Spirit (7:39). There is possibly a symbolic or secondary allusion in John 19:34 to the new life we gain through the death of Christ and its atoning efficacy;

(3) the primary point of John 19.34 is that the spear thrust and outflow of blood and water prove Jesus' actual physical nature and death. That this is the main point is made clear by the quotations that follow in verses 36-37.

The allusions to Exodus 12:46 and Numbers 9:12, as Beasley-Murray says,

> relate to the Passover Lamb, for Jesus in His dying fulfilled that type of redemption. . . . The interest in the blood and water is subordinate to the major motif of Jesus as God's Passover Lamb. Nevertheless . . . the efflux of blood and water from the body of Jesus reveals his true humanity and disposes of the contentions of the Docetists, who denied that the Christ had a body of flesh and blood and died.[6]

Nothing is to be learned here about water baptism except perhaps for a very subsidiary motif that both sacraments spring from and symbolize Jesus' atoning death. But I doubt our author has even this in mind. His interests lie decidedly elsewhere in his incarnational theology. Jesus truly came, he truly died, and to deny "Jesus Christ come in the flesh," as he will point out in 1 John, is to affirm that one is not a Christian at all. The purpose statement in John 20:30-31 reminds one and all that this gospel is written so that one might begin to believe that the historical Jesus is also the Christ, the Son of the Living God come in the flesh. Christology, not sacramental theology, is what this gospel is all about.

FIRST JOHN 5:5-8: THE TALE OF THREE WITNESSES

The context of 1 John 5:5-8 is crucial to understanding this text.[7] The author of 1 John, who may be the same as the author of the Fourth Gospel,[8] is proceeding along lines that we have already seen in the Gospel of John. Incarnational theology is being offered to combat docetic tendencies. Thus, in 1 John 4:3, we read: "Every spirit that acknowledges that Jesus Christ came in the flesh from God. . . ." Again, we have the phrase "Everyone who believes that Jesus is the Christ born of God . . ." (5:1). Immediately preceding the text under consideration, we find yet another attempt to drive home the Incarnation: "Only he who believes that Jesus is the Son of God . . ." (5:5). In short, he who affirms that the man Jesus was also Christ, the Son of God, is a Christian. Everyone denying the Incarnation does not have the Spirit of God and is not a Christian.

The first point of exegesis that is important is that 5:6 says, "This is the one who came . . . ," and not, "This is the one who comes." A past historical event is in view, not something in the present. Thus, this verse cannot refer to the Christian sacraments. Two possibilities are available for the meaning of "This is the one who came through (or by) water and blood"; it may refer to Jesus' baptism and his death.[9] We would then see a close connection once again between Jesus' baptism and his death, so that perhaps we are meant to see one in the light of the other. More likely, however, as with John 3:5, water refers here to Jesus' physical birth, blood to his physical death. This interpretation makes sense in light of 1 John 4:3, 5:1, and 5:5, and it is more to the point.

The next sentence, "He did not come only by water, but by water and blood," emphasizes, under my interpretation, not only that Jesus took on a human nature, but also that he was so associated with human flesh that he experienced the utmost indication of its reality, its weakness, and its contingency—physical death. This statement does an excellent job of driving home the point of Jesus' humanity.

The sentence that follows reads: "[I]t is the Spirit who testifies," and reveals how we know these facts about the humanity of Jesus. Even the gift "from above" testifies to the real human nature of Jesus. Then follows, "For there are three that testify, the Spirit, the water, the blood, and the three are in agreement." Many have seen a reference to the sacraments and the Spirit here, but we are told that this is God's testimony about his Son (v. 9). Further, as Dunn says, "It is a fact that αἷμα by itself is never used in the New Testament as a designation of the Lord's Supper." He goes on to say, "The Spirit bears witness to the Son of God, to Jesus Christ, to him who came by water and blood—not merely to two events in his earthly life."[10] From this, however, Dunn does not draw the proper conclusion. Jesus' water baptism was a contingent, though important, event that John's gospel never mentions directly, but only alludes to in John 1:29ff.

Since 1 John as a discourse is dependent on the themes we also find in the gospel, one would expect no more reference here to water baptism than there. But, more importantly, while Jesus' water baptism was important as the beginning of his ministry and indicates his assuming the role of representative and servant, it is not an event that is the best aid in arguing for the Incarnation.

True, it might show that Jesus, a human being, would go through baptism like all of us, but it proves too much. I think the Fourth Gospel writer did not explicitly mention Jesus' baptism precisely because it might imply Jesus' need for repentance or the remission of sins. This negative truth about humanity is not what the gospel writer or the author of 1 John wanted to relate about Jesus' humanity. Such a mention in so theologically a loaded gospel as this one might leave the wrong impression about the weight and significance of water baptism.

More likely, the things that bear witness are not contingent events, but those things that, in Johannine theology, are eternal events, once for all—the Incarnation and the death, and of course the Holy Spirit. They still testify to us because they are eternal and eternally significant. In verse 8, the Spirit is mentioned first because in Christian experience it is through his testimony that we know the eternal truths about the Son of God. Because the Spirit is true (v. 6) the Spirit brings with it what it testifies about—the reality and presence of the Incarnate, dead, risen Son of God (cf. John 15:26, 16:14, 14:16-17, and especially 14:23). Thus, the believer has both the testimony and the Testifier in him (5: 10-12) as part of his own physical and spiritual reality.

First John 5:5-8 speaks powerfully about the Son of God, who was the man Jesus born of flesh; died in the flesh; and testified to, in, and by the Spirit in the believer. This language may be said to be reminiscent of sacramentalism, but the discussion is not about symbols but of the realities they depict in the Son of God. Accordingly, while we may affirm the sacramental language in the Johannine literature and may even see a possible subsidiary allusion to the sacraments in John 19:34, this literature tells us a great deal in a magnificent way about Jesus who was the Christ "come in human flesh," about the connection of the physical and the spiritual, and about the reality of the death of the Son of God. It tells us little or nothing about Christian water baptism, however, except perhaps how well its language evokes the realities of salvation history to which it points, and how successfully it serves as a sign that points to something other than itself. If we are to garner anything from the discussion of John 1–3—with its absence of reference to Jesus' own baptism; its discussion of how water of purification cannot bring life to the party, but the new wine (of Jesus) can; and finally how the waters associated with birth only bring one into the world, but not into the world to come—one can only conclude that material "water" is not the substance on which this evangelist wants us to focus our attention. In fact, we must get beyond the lifeless water to get to the spiritual living water that comes not from the sacrament but from Jesus himself. As always, this evangelist is talking to his audience on two levels, and only the higher and spiritual discourse and realities lead to new birth, new life, new wine, and a new covenant.

Chapter 6

DOWN IN THE FLOOD

Baptism in Hebrews and 1 Peter

The epistle to the Hebrews is a document steeped in Old Testament theology and ethics. Whomever its author may be, its audience seems almost certainly to have been Jewish Christians who could appreciate the many subtleties of Old Testament principle and practice expounded in the light of Christ.[1] Possibly the author was aware of such Jewish practices as proselyte baptism, but in any case he was certainly familiar with various Old Testament lustrations for impurity.

LEAVING YOUR LUSTRATIONS BEHIND: HEBREWS 6:1-6

The first passage of interest is Hebrews 6:1-6, long a conundrum for those of the Reformed faith because of verse 4-6. Our interests, however, lie elsewhere in this discussion.

In this passage, the author is reminding his audience about the elementary teachings in a passing way, because he is urging his audience to "go on to maturity" (6:1). The group of things he includes as part of Christian foundations are "repentance from acts that lead to death, and of faith in God, instructions about baptisms (or washings), the laying on of hands, the resurrection of the dead and eternal judgment" (6:1-2). These things deal with a Christian's beginnings, or the beginnings of becoming a Christian, which include matters of rites, theology, and ethics. As Dunn notes, all these matters are shared in common between Judaism and Christianity, and it is likely that this sort of overlapping foundation was the kind used as an apologetic and technique to lead Jews to Christ, for "they are the points at which the Christian evangel to Jews would begin, the points which the evangelist would then elaborate in specifically Christian terms."[2]

This fact probably gives a clue to the puzzling plural *baptisms*, which can of course be translated "washings," but if, as I am inclined to think, the author is Apollos, then quite likely he means John's baptism as well as Christian baptism. At the very least, Christian baptism is likely one of the kinds of baptism to which the author is referring. The other probably is not Spirit Baptism, which was not an idea that early Jewish and Christian literature shares in common. As I have hinted, we could translate the word as "washings" or "cleansing" and see in it a general term referring to various sorts of lustrations, perhaps not including Christian baptism but only Jewish ceremonial washings. This approach could find support in Hebrews 9:10 and perhaps elsewhere in the New Testament (Mark 7:14, and perhaps Col 2:12 in a variant reading).

If this approach is correct, then the rite of proselyte baptism possibly was associated with Christian baptism not only in the minds of those addressed, but also in the mind of the epistle's author. This conclusion is only a conjecture from which one should build little, but it is worth pondering. It would have some implications for the background of infant baptism as a Christian practice.

To return to our text, we note the close connection for one's future between repentance, faith, baptisms, laying on of hands, and the theological implications of commitment to Christ. We see that for adult converts from Judaism, the initiation-conversion process was likely compressed into a small span of time. This probably was the normal state of affairs in the early church when both Jews and Gentiles were entering the community of Christians from the outside (unlike Christian children), with a religious background and upbringing that was not specifically Christian, and was likely in some ways anti-Christian. This descriptive statement then tells us a good deal of how things were done, and perhaps how they should be done today when people with similar backgrounds (non-Christians) are involved. The matter of laying on of hands may refer to Spirit Baptism (cf. Acts 8:19, 19:1ff.), and in any case the whole process seems to be thought of here as virtually one ceremony.[3] In addition, there is probably no reference to water baptism in 6:4-5, but only to various ways of describing the Spirit's work in the believer, as Dunn and others have suggested. As the author says in Hebrews 6:1, we ought to leave the elementary things behind, and not focus on them as mature Christian persons. He also makes clear that water baptism is one of those initiatory and elementary things that one encounters at the beginning of the initiation-conversion process.

HEBREWS 10:22-23: WASHED WITH PURE WATER, SPRINKLED WITHIN

In this passage we have a reference to both spiritual and internal cleansing, as well as physical washing in water baptism. That the two are mentioned together probably indicates that water baptism for the author of the letter to the Hebrews symbolized spiritual cleansing, the washing clean of a guilty conscience (cf. below on 1 Pet 3:21). The reference to "pure" water has as its background either "the water for impurity" (cf. Num 19:9, 17ff., Lev 16:6, 16, and Heb 9:13), or some text such as Ezekiel 36:25. The author does not say that the internal cleansing is by the external rite; in fact, he distinguishes them by a coordinate conjunction *and*, while recognizing that the two things are similar or parallel. No *ex opere operato* view of water baptism appears here; it is a rite that only washes the body with pure water. As a closing comment on this passage we may quote Dunn:

The close complementary nature of the two cleansings (of heart and body) remind us that we cannot separate Christian baptism from conversion. It is related to the cleansing of the heart as the body is related to the heart. It is the outward embodiment of the spiritual transformation which is taking place inside a man. It would simply not occur to the writer, or to early Christians generally, that the two could be separate. *The popular idea that conversion precedes baptism, and that baptism is a confession of a commitment made some time previously is not to be found in the New Testament. Baptism is the act of faith, part of the total cleansing which enables the convert to draw near and to enter the Holy of Holies by the way opened up for him by Jesus (vv. 11-22).*[4]

If Dunn is right, then he has swiftly ruled out both Paedo-Baptist and Baptist practice as usually exercised in the church today. I am not denying that what he says is true for those proselytes entering the community of faith from backgrounds similar to those of the audience of the letter to the Hebrews. Nor am I denying that this may be true in similar situations in the church today. But if Dunn is going to insist on the order water then Spirit as normative, then it appears that he sees water baptism as a means for a sincere candidate, willing to repent and believe (or at least to begin to do so and submit to the water rite), to make God an offer God cannot refuse.

This view of Spirit Baptism with water baptism in the end differs little from an *ex opere operato* view, if in fact the Spirit really does come virtually at the same time the water is poured on the candidate. Thus, this view states that God must give the Spirit since it comes with water baptism if the candidate's heart and confession are right. This view, which I call occasionalism—by which I mean that the two things are thought to occur on or at the same occasion—is found in a slightly different form in Beasley-Murray's study. I do not think that Dunn can draw such a conclusion on the basis of Hebrews 10:22-23. The two patterns of water then Spirit and Spirit then water found in Acts should warn us against such thinking. Presumably Dunn would argue, as in

Acts 8, that though one may believe and be baptized, and the Spirit may not come until later, this is abnormal. But is this really so?

The view of Dunn and Beasley-Murray on this matter, while having much to commend it if one is discussing a strictly missionary baptism, has little to commend it when one tries to apply it to the church of even a few generations after New Testament times. For one thing, such a tightly knit conversion-initiation scheme overlooks the obvious fact that many Christians were converted and received the Spirit quite apart from Christian water initiation. More to the point, it ignores the fact that for many Christians today and in the past, and especially those of Christian parents (Baptist or Paedo-Baptist), the conversion process has been a slow one, lasting over a period of months or years. Many people in such situations have been converted and received the Spirit not in a dramatic event, but through a quiet inner revolution. Many cannot point to one instant or even a day when they were brought dramatically from the darkness into light. This is partly a result of a greater familiarity with Christianity as part of our very environment. It is also partly a result of Christian families. Dunn and Beasley-Murray err in taking a part (one sort of conversion-initiation experience) and trying to argue for a whole when it manifestly is not. This is indeed the danger in taking descriptive statements about how some people were in New Testament times initiated into the faith, and trying to apply them to all and sundry. The fact is, to our condemnation, the Christian faith today in the Western world is not so much a missionary religion as it ought to be, and as it was in New Testament times. As a result, we do not see enough of the sort of tightly knit conversion-initiation experiences that are recorded in Acts and elsewhere in the New Testament.

The solution to this problem is more missionary efforts, not castigating attempts to adapt and adopt New Testament teaching on water baptism for later generations and Christian family situations. More will be said on this point later. The church does need reform all around, but the answer is not to be found in squeezing it into one very narrow pattern, which is not even the only pattern found in the New Testament.

FIRST PETER 3:21: DOWN IN THE FLOOD WITH NOAH

It has long been argued that 1 Peter is a baptismal treatise, and thus it is only appropriate that we should end our exegetical study with an excerpt from this letter. In fact, however, few if any of the commentaries written in the last twenty years on 1 Peter still see 1 Peter that way.[5] Perhaps the most frequent assertion was that 1:3–4:11 reflects the pattern the author of 1 Peter advocated or followed in baptismal instruction.[6] There is little doubt that the language and symbolism of water baptism permeate this epistle, but we have only one real reference to the rite itself, in 3:21. Unfortunately our text and its context are fraught with exegetical and theological difficulties.

On its face, this text appears to be talking about baptism as an *ex opere operato* rite that saves in some magical way, yet this hardly comports with what is said about salvation elsewhere in this letter (cf. 1:3, 5, 9, 23, for instance). In 1 Peter 3:20 we are told about Noah and his experience with the flood. God waited patiently while Noah built the ark; God withheld his judgment while the ark was built so that a few might be saved. In fact, the text says that eight were saved in Noah's family. Paradoxically enough, many were condemned, but some were saved. To use Meredith Kline's terminology, it was a redemptive-judgment executing God's vindication and vengeance in a single act. Here was a trial by water ordeal on a massive scale, as was noted in chapter 1. Salvation was on the basis of the household principle in this Old Testament event. There is some question about the phrase δι᾽ ὕδατος at the end of verse 20. Does it mean they were kept safe as they passed "through" the waters (local sense), or they were kept safe "by means of" the waters (instrumental sense), or some combination of the two? I incline to the view that while Noah was kept safe as he passed through the water and this might be in the background here, more like we should take the phrase in an instrumental sense. This interpretation fits what follows better and also the idea present in verse 20 of God's simultaneous redemptive-judgment.[7] We are now prepared to examine 3:21. Straightway we face a serious difficulty of a textual nature. It is possible that the first word of verse 21 is ὅ would refer back to the flood water and be translated "which." Other manuscripts either have omitted the word or have used ἥ for ὅς. By far the best support in terms of strength of evidence and witness goes with the first possibility, and furthermore it is by far the more difficult reading, and thus to be preferred.[8] We should translate the sentence as follows: "eight were saved by means of the water, the antitype of which saves you now—baptism."

Here we are thrust into the dark waters of typology. The principle of typology is simple, though its outworkings can be complex. It operates on the assumption that God works in a pattern, a regular pattern, so that "what he has done in the past, as recorded in the Old Testament, can be expected to find its counterpart in his work in the decisive period of the New Testament."[9] Thus, the author of this epistle sees Christian baptism as an antitype not of salvation through the flood, but the flood itself.[10] Baptism then represents something similar to what its Old Testament model was—an act of divine redemptive-judgment. This is significant, and once again we have baptism associated with death or divine judgment, a water ordeal, but a saving death or judgment. The act in New Testament times that was the counterpart of the flood is, of course, the death of Christ which was God's judgment on sinful humanity, and yet also his salvation of some of the same sinful persons as they aligned themselves with their Savior.

Here again Christian baptism represents divine redemptive-judgment. It is a sign of the cutting off of sinful persons, the washing clean of the earth, but at the same time and in the same act it saves human beings. In what sense does baptism save us? We are told only at the end of the verse: "through the resurrection of Jesus Christ." Thus, we are saved by the divine redemptive-judgment of God, symbolized in baptism, only because after Christ died (the manifestation of this judgment), he also rose from the dead, triumphing over death. Looking backwards, we are saved by the death of Christ, but only through his resurrection, which made that act of judgment also redemptive. As Paul puts it, "If Christ has not been raised, then your faith is futile; you are still in your sins" (1 Cor 15:17). I am not saying that an explicit reference to Christ's death appears here, but by saying that baptism is an antitype of the flood that saved Noah, and by mentioning the resurrection, I think this is clearly implied. In the midst of the explanation of how baptism saves, we are given two clauses which, though they relate to the matter of how baptism saves, are more a definition of what baptism is—"not the removal of dirt from the flesh, but the appeal unto God for a good conscience (or possibly a Christian life)." The grammar at this point is difficult, but baptism is the last word before these two clauses and logically they explain what baptism is, not so much how it saves. The "how" is explained by the διά clause at the end of the verse.

If the first of these two clauses was a διὰ clause explaining how or by what means baptism saves, then we could say that the "removal" clause removes the possibility that baptism works *ex opere operato*. I think that such a view of baptism is ruled out not by this clause but by the διὰ clause at the end of the verse. To say baptism or what it represents (divine redemptive-judgment) saves us through the resurrection is probably to make clear that it does not operate magically. Rather, only as we appropriate the resurrection in our lives is our baptism validated and what it represents saved (cf. 1:3).

What then does this first clause define baptism as not being? The language is difficult. That the author is saying "baptism does not clean the body" does not seem likely, because that is to deny the one thing that water baptism actually does do in the physical realm! The word for "removal" suggests a physical putting away and is certainly a strange verb to use to describe a washing. Rather, the word suggests a physical putting away, like the taking off of one's clothes or of some impediment (cf. its only other New Testament use, 2 Peter 1:14, which refers to the shedding of the physical body at death). This phrase quite possibly refers to circumcision. In Judaism, the foreskin was considered an unclean part of the body.[11] The word *removal* here is apt if circumcision is in view.[12] It seems likely that Peter is contrasting baptism and circumcision, the two signs of redemptive-judgment, of cutting off and yet grafting in.[13] Perhaps here, as in Colossians 2:11, the parallel natures or functions for the two rites are being recognized, but here especially we are told that baptism is not circumcision, and probably because of the way in which circumcision is expressed, he means that baptism is not just an outer physical cleansing, a removal of dirt from the body. This phrase is ambiguous enough to conjure up circumcision, but it also reminds one of baptism.

The next clause then explains what baptism is. Baptism is an inquiry, appeal, or pledge of, or for, a good conscience, or a Christian life. In regard to the first word, it can mean the asking of a question. In fact, this is what it usually means in verbal form. On one occasion the verb for "inquiry" means a request (Matthew 16:12). Could baptism be an inquiry or appeal unto God? In fact, it could be. In Acts we noted that Paul was told to be baptized, calling on the Lord (22:16). Water baptism might be seen as an appeal to God for the Spirit or for the ability to live a Christian life. Remember that we are talking of what baptism, the act itself, is, not what may accompany it. Thus, we are not talking of an appeal or a pledge of faithfulness that went along with the rite, but the rite itself.

If we are to follow what the Greek ἐπερώτημα word means in the papyri, we should perhaps translate it as a "pledge," "contract," or "undertaking."[14] This second possibility fits the Old Testament parallel, for circumcision was a sign of a pledge of covenant loyalty and faithfulness to Yahweh. This latter suggestion is accepted by most commentators as more likely, though the former cannot be ruled out. The second phrase may refer to a "good conscience" as it is so often translated, and thus may mean that this text is similar to Hebrews 10:22. The lengthy study by Christian Maurer, however, probably is to be followed here, and he concludes that this phrase in the post-Pauline literature is a formula for the Christian life.[15] Thus, our definition of baptism reads as follows: "Baptism is not circumcision, but an appeal or pledge unto God for a Christian life." The baptized then appeals not from one's own good conscience, but to God, that he or she may lead a Christian life henceforth.

Baptism is an act that saves only in that it recognizes that God alone saves through the resurrection of Christ, and God alone gives one the grace to lead a Christian life. But the baptized, trusting in these things, pledges to God the Christian life he or she at the same time appeals for. Baptism is the first step in the undertaking of a Christian life; it is a contract or covenanting with God who "gives what He commands, and then commands whatsoever He wills," as Augustine suggested. Baptism is a sign of a covenant—a sign that, like circumcision, vividly depicts divine redemptive-judgment. Unlike circumcision, which has become a mere external cleansing now that the new covenant has begun, baptism is not only an external rite. The act itself is an appeal or pledge to God for a Christian life; an appeal or pledge made through the resurrection, and thus it can be an appeal or pledge that saves because the God who gave this sign of covenanting keeps his promise. If it is implied that, as with Noah, so with the baptized, God saves on the basis of the household principle, then one could argue that one should administer the sign of that salvation to one's own household, even one's infants. However, we are told that baptism is not like circumcision in this very text. Thus, to press this text to answer the question of infant baptism is probably wrong, especially as it does not deal with the question directly.

We have come a long way in our study in a short span of time, and now we are at the point where we can pull the pieces together and ask: what would a New Testament theology of baptism actually look like if it took all the evidence and contexts into consideration? We save that synthetic discussion for our final chapter, but here we should note that in fact there is not nearly so much evidence about water baptism in the New Testament as we might like. The authors of the New Testament books were not mainly—one might even say not greatly—concerned about this matter. When one eliminates all the metaphorical use of baptismal language that is not really discussing the rite of baptism itself, then only a few key passages are available to help us.

We have no absolutely clear guidance on the mode of baptism in the New Testament, no clear guidance on whether water baptism must precede Spirit Baptism or follow it, though the former pattern seems more in evidence, and once one has the Spirit, Acts 10 suggests that there should be no delay in receiving water baptism. The analogies that we have with circumcision or ancient water ordeals or Jewish proselyte baptism are indeed helpful, but the analogies with mystery religions and pagan rituals turn out to be of no use at all. Baptism is not about resurrection, nor even about dying and rising, to judge from Romans 6.

I say all this to draw one salient conclusion at the close of this chapter that ends the detailed discussion of passages: it is no wonder that we have been debating baptism for two thousand years now, with no sign of the debating abating. The New Testament does not answer all of our modern questions about baptism, and it especially does not answer questions about what to do with Christian children when it comes to baptism. As Dunn said earlier, the popular notion that conversion necessarily precedes baptism and should be seen as a seal or testimony or even a confession to conversion and commitment previously made is nowhere clearly stated in the New Testament.

Unfortunately, baptism is one of those contentious issues that pushes us so that we cannot and do not allow the silences in the New Testament text to rest in peace. We fill in the gaps with our own theologies and urgencies, which has led to turning baptism into something it is not: a Christian infant dedication ritual, or a Christian bar mitzvah or confirmation ritual. This result is understandable, because the church today is mainly a nurture organization which has a missionary committee or two. If it were rather a missionary movement that also did nurture, I suspect we would read Acts and the other New Testament evidence quite differently, for what we see in the New Testament reflects the missionary situation, not a settled system of church and sacraments. Most of all, if the New Testament teaches us anything on this subject, it is that we should be prepared for surprises and divine irregularities, and we should accept that Acts tells us that sometimes water baptism comes before, sometimes with, and sometimes after the Spirit has baptized a person into Christ. God can do it how God wants to do it when it comes to salvation. We are playing catch-up ball. And this memo just in: We humans cannot control the liberating grace of God through the sacraments. We are not in charge of such things. We need to stop thinking we are.

Chapter 7

A RITE OF PASSAGE

A Theology of Water Baptism in the New Testament

SIGN, SACRAMENT, OR SEAL?

We have indirectly been asking in this study the age-old question of whether water baptism is a sacrament, sign, seal, or possibly some combination of the three. We can now answer this question to some degree, but we must keep one thing in mind. A person's theology of baptism is to one degree or another a function of a person's soteriology—one's theology of salvation. If one thinks salvation comes in stages such that one can say I have been saved (at conversion), I am being saved (now through the sanctifying work of the Spirit), and I will be saved (eschatological salvation in which one is fully conformed to Christ's image when he returns and raises believers from the dead), one is not likely to think that water baptism in itself either "saves" or symbolizes the whole of salvation. One is more likely to think it only symbolizes the initial work of God in salvation—regeneration.

But of course this still does not settle the matter, because in some classic Protestant models of salvation, regeneration follows repentance and the initial embracing of Christ in faith, while in other models of salvation regeneration precedes and enables repentance and faith. Precisely because the theology of water baptism is an extension of one's theology of salvation, those who tend to think that regeneration follows things like repentance and initial faith are likely to think that baptism should follow confession of faith. The problem with this whole model is that it is not really what the New Testament says about regeneration. Regeneration is simply the negative or distaff side of conversion, what enables a true profession of faith. Whether one sees this as a result of the individual responding positively to the prevenient grace of God or as a function of God's electing grace, in either model one will not be disposed to see water baptism as either a sign or a means of our response to salvation. Rather, one will see baptism as symbolizing some sort of work of God in or for the believer. But let us put this in more biblical terms.

For Paul, the primary difference between the Abrahamic covenant and the new covenant was that of their relative relationship to the key events in salvation history (cf. Rom 4; Gal 3). The new covenant stands on this side of the crucial death-resurrection-Spirit-giving of Jesus Christ, while the Abrahamic covenant stands on the other side of the great divide. Thus, while Abraham experienced the promise given, Christians experience the reception of the promised Spirit. We see here a relationship of promise and fulfillment, though even we have only begun to experience the salvation God has to give us. I surmise that it is because of this relationship of promise and fulfillment that Paul, while calling circumcision both a sign and seal (Rom 4:11), calls only the Spirit the seal of the new covenant.

Because we live in the age of the beginning of the fulfillment, the age between ascension and Parousia, to call the sign of the covenant its seal as well is no longer appropriate. We experience what the sign signifies, what the prophet Joel foresaw—the thing itself, the baptism, or the pouring out of the Spirit, which ratifies the covenant in our lives; the Spirit alone gives us assurance of our full salvation, while providing the initial and sanctifying work that allows us to say, "I have been saved and am being saved." Because the reality has come to us, the covenant sign should no longer be called by that name appropriate for the thing itself. Water baptism then, is not the seal of the new covenant, though it is still the sign of the promise. It is the sign of the seal, but not the sign that is the seal. Thus, water baptism differs from circumcision in that it only prepares one for the seal.

This preparatory nature of water baptism also leads one to question whether or not calling it a sacrament is appropriate, if we mean by this an outward and visible sign of an inward and spiritual grace that is conveyed through, with, or by water baptism. If one accepts the view of Dunn or Beasley-Murray that water baptism is the occasion for the giving of the Spirit, then undoubtedly the term *sacrament* in the sense mentioned above might still be appropriate. Dunn, however, after going to great pains to distinguish water baptism and Spirit Baptism and to show that this distinction is present in the New Testament, then says that it would not have occurred to the New Testament writers the two types of baptism could be separate.[1] This I find stunning. I think Dunn has shown clearly that the two baptisms, while related as sign and thing signified, were distinguished in the New Testament, and probably no one imposed or thought in terms of a normative time gap or lack thereof between them. That the writer of Hebrews can speak of water baptism and Spirit Baptism together (10:22) is because of their close logical and theological relationship and, so far as I can see, that no time scheme need be implied by such a statement. If there is one, however, it is certainly not made explicit.

In Latin, the word *sacramentum* originally meant an oath of allegiance. If 1 Peter 3:21 should be translated in terms of a pledge, then water baptism is a sacrament in this sense. Undoubtedly, in traditional Baptist theology water baptism will continue to be thought of as a sacrament in this sense. But suppose one wishes to derive sacrament from the Greek term μυστήριον (from which we get the word *mystery*). Suppose one wants to see in water baptism a picture of the mystery or sacrament of Spirit Baptism, a picture of the death of Christ as well as of the sinner's old nature, and finally a picture of our burial with Christ and cleansing through the Spirit: Then I am content to call baptism a sacrament. Baptism is indeed, as has been said so often, a visible word, the gospel for the eyes, but like the parables it has a quality of being veiled or mysterious so that only those who have eyes may see this visible word for what it is.

Water baptism is first and foremost a sign, a powerful symbol that evokes the realities of salvation history in the life of Christ, and of the believer. In fact, it was such a powerful symbol that its language permeates the similes and metaphors of initiation and conversion in the New Testament. While the foundations of water baptism are the death, resurrection, and Spirit giving of Jesus, only the first and last of these are shadowed forth in water baptism. Perhaps the authors of the New Testament deliberately avoided the idea of baptism as a dying and rising because of its pagan associations, but for whatever reason, water baptism does not depict either Christ's resurrection or ours.

ASSEMBLING THE SYMBOL

Let us briefly review what water baptism symbolizes. The most obvious thing is spiritual washing (Heb 10:23, Acts 22:16, and the language of water baptism in Eph 5:26-27). It is a striking fact that the most dominant image that comes to the mind of New Testament writers when they think of water baptism is death, and not just any sort of death, but a death that is a judgment of God. Nor is it simply a matter of judgment, but rather a redemptive-judgment. Sometimes this is a matter of drawing on ideas about Old Testament water ordeals or the Old Testament covenant sign; sometimes it is a matter of specifically drawing on the atoning death of Jesus. In 1 Peter 3:21, for instance, baptism is the antitype of the flood, a redemptive-judgment of God in which many perished though Noah and his family were saved. In 1 Corinthians 10:1ff., the Red Sea crossing is the "type" of baptism, the event through which the Jews were saved and the Egyptians drowned in another act of God. Paul even says what happened to the Jews then is that they were baptized into Moses (without being immersed in water!).

In 1 Peter 3:21, baptism is not said to be circumcision, while in Colossians 2:11, baptism is associated closely with the circumcision of Christ and his death, in which we who are in Christ have been circumcised. In both Romans 6:1ff. and Colossians 2:11, baptism is said to be our burial with Christ. In 1 Corinthians 1:13 also there is a close association of baptism and crucifixion. The one who suffered the latter is the one who commissioned and is named with the former. Jesus' own experience of John's baptism and his description of his own death as a baptism may have led to this close association of baptism and death, as well as baptism and judgment (cf. Matt 3:15; Mark 10:38, Luke 12:50).

It seems likely that at least one of the reasons water baptism is said to be "one" (Eph 4:5) is its strong associations with Christ's death, which is a once-for-all-time event. Perhaps its associations with the one Spirit Baptism also had something to do with this. The association between water baptism and Spirit Baptism in Paul is mainly a linguistic one. Such texts as 1 Corinthians 6:11, Ephesians 5:25-27, Galatians 3:26-28, and 1 Corinthians 12:13 indicate that for Paul the water baptismal act symbolized a greater and internal circumcision and cleansing, baptizing and incorporating into Christ through the Spirit. This unification through the Spirit had a specific moral effect and implication: one had died to sin (Rom 6:2) and one was to continue to reckon oneself dead to sin (Rom 6:11). This is part of the already–not yet state of our sanctification, and why in much of Paul's ethics he is saying, "Be (become) what you already are" (to borrow the words of Rudolf Bultmann).

The fact that the act of water baptism or its language used to describe Spirit Baptism, cleansing, or unification in Christ is present in ethical contexts really does not prove what Barth so strongly argued. It does not prove that water baptism was seen by Paul as essentially an ethical act, or even the first ethical act of the Christian. For instance, we note in Romans 6:1ff. Paul appeals to both water baptism and Spirit Baptism in order to urge the Romans to continue being dead to sin. No one would argue that Paul's appeal to Spirit Baptism to support his ethical enjoinder meant that Spirit Baptism was seen as an ethical act. On the contrary, Spirit Baptism was the supremely and uniquely divine act.

THE TWO BAPTISMS: WATER AND SPIRIT

Sometimes scholars, being the pedantic sorts they are, point out that we do not have in the New Testament the noun phrase *the baptism of the Holy Spirit.* This claim is true enough but irrelevant, since the idea is so clearly present in texts like 1 Corinthians 12:13. In order to be absolutely clear at this juncture about the two baptisms, I am not arguing that water baptism is a divine act. Rather, it is essentially a community act on behalf of the baptized. Water baptism, like Spirit baptism, is never described as an action of the one being baptized, for it is never found in the active voice or the middle voice (with the possible exception of Acts 22:16) when the verb is used and the baptized is the subject. This should tell us something about whether or not water baptism is seen as inherently an ethical act of the baptized.

The association of water baptism and Spirit Baptism and their interrelation as acts is more visible in the book of Acts. We saw two patterns in Acts: (1) water then (2) Spirit (2:38, 19:5-6; cf. Matt 28:19-20), which seems to be the more normal order, and Spirit then water (8:37, 16:14-15, 32-33, 11:17). In the latter case, the thinking was that water baptism should take place as soon after Spirit Baptism as possible, for who can refuse someone the sign of the divine promise when he or she has already received the thing signified, the seal that is the Spirit? As Dunn recognized, this should have implications for the Baptist churches of today. What we do not find in Acts is the pattern Spirit with water or vice versa (though Paul's case may suggest that "occasionalism" was sometimes the case). This should lead us to question any *ex opere operato* view of water baptism—any automatic dispensing of grace through or by water baptism. Spirit Baptism was almost always prior or subsequent to water baptism, usually in very close sequence in Acts. That the two baptisms were never synonymous is clear.

In regard to the antecedents of water baptism, we argued that John's baptism had the most likelihood of affecting Christian practice. We saw such an effect in Peter's preaching in Acts 2:38, and we may compare also Acts 11:16, in which something important comes to light. Peter clearly sees Jesus' Spirit Baptism as a contrast to water baptism (note the δέ ["but"] also present in the gospels). What this means is that if Peter saw Christian water baptism as like John's water baptism, then he more likely saw it also in contrast to Christian Spirit Baptism as something preparatory for receiving the Kingdom or Spirit Baptism. It appears, however, that Peter borrowed the associations of repentance before or in the act of water baptism for a forgiveness of sins that was to be received subsequently (Acts 2:38, cf. Mark 1:4). Christian baptism was also something different from John's baptism; it was an act on the basis of Jesus' death-resurrection-Spirit-giving and thus done in his name, probably as an appeal to that Name who did these things. The point would be to ask the dead and risen Savior to apply the fruits of these events to the baptized by giving the Spirit. As Jesus' own water baptism was associated with a prayer that likely was an appeal to the Father (Luke 3:21), this perhaps affected the way water baptism was viewed later by the church. Acts 22:16 reveals that an appeal to the Lord's name was associated with water baptism. First Peter 3:21 may mean that the very act of water baptism was an appeal for a Christian life, though the meaning may be that baptism is a pledge or promise to lead a Christian life.

KNOWN BY THE COMPANY IT KEEPS

Besides the aspect of an appeal, certain other things are often associated with the water rite in the New Testament. In Acts, for instance, while we could find no evidence of an emphasis on confession of faith with or before water baptism (except in the noncanonical text of Acts 8:37), there was a frequent association of the act with the preaching of the gospel, a call to believe, or a call to repent. While they may have made some sort of verbal repentance, it appears that, at least in

the case of the Samaritans of Acts 8 or the Jews of Acts 2, the willingness to be baptized was taken as the indication of reception of God's
word. Sometimes in Acts we are told that they believed or received the
Word and were baptized (cf. 16:14-15), but we are not told how this
was known to the baptizers, or whether or not anything was said by the
baptized before the rite. In Paul, we saw a different pattern.

Except for Ephesians 4:5, which is a confession about faith and
water baptism among other things but which gives no indication as
to how Paul related faith and the water rite with confession (as even
Dunn admitted), there is nowhere a close association of water baptism
to faith in this apostle's writings. There is an extraordinarily frequent
assertion of water baptism as sign, and of the spiritual reality as thing
signified, as in Romans 6 and Colossians 2. As part of this connection,
Paul also associates water baptism and our spiritual circumcision in
the circumcising death of Christ by means of the Spirit.

In view of such texts as Acts 15:1ff. and 21:20ff., it is evident that
among Jewish Christians circumcision and water baptism were being
practiced side by side,[2] and the latter was not seen as the replacement
of the former. So much was this the case that Paul had to write to the
Galatians to fight off the attempt to circumcise even the Gentiles who
were converting and being baptized. Paul himself was probably the first
to see the water rite as the replacement of circumcision as a sign, and
to see Jesus' death and our spiritual circumcision as the fulfillment of
the old covenant sign. Undoubtedly, the Jerusalem Jewish Christians
had seen circumcision as a sign that they would continue, to obey the
only written Scriptures then available, and particularly the Mosaic Law
(cf. Acts 21:20 and Gal 3-4). To them, baptism did not contradict this
allegiance since it was a baptism in the name of the Jewish Messiah. By
circumcision, one pledged to obey God's law, while by water baptism,
one recognized Jesus as the one foretold in that Law.

Paul clearly saw the problems that circumcision created for the
Gentiles. There was no need (indeed, Paul thought it was wrong) to ask
Gentiles to become good Jews first before becoming good Christians.
The basis of the new covenant is faith in the promises of God and

nothing more. Accordingly, Paul himself appears to have developed the idea and practice of water baptism as the rite replacing circumcision, implying that before Paul did this, there was no thought of infant baptism unless proselyte baptism among Jews involved this action and it was affecting the Christian rite. Hebrews 6 may imply such an association with proselyte baptism, but it is too slender a thread with which to weave a firm conclusion.

Having said this, did Paul himself work out the implications of his parallels between the Abrahamic covenant and the new covenant, between circumcision and water baptism, in such a way that he accepted or even administered infant baptism? It is not impossible, especially when one remembers that many of Paul's converts were Jews (or proselytes of Judaism, or God-fearers) who would expect or even ask for some rite for their infants and especially those born after their parent's conversions who were not now to be circumcised because of Paul's dictum. There is no clear evidence that Paul did baptize infants, but 1 Corinthians 7:14, 10:1ff., or 15:29 might imply that he would not rule out such a thing. If he was prepared to allow proxy baptism for the Christian dead, one would think he wouldn't have a problem with administering it to any of the living within the circle of the new covenant community.

If he had reflected on it, Paul possibly would have argued that a holy child, by virtue of the grace of God working through the Christian parent or parents, was set apart for God and thus should receive the sign that signifies the setting apart of Christ's people from everyone else. That many later deduced such things is understandable. Again, however, there is no evidence that Paul baptized children, and even the house baptisms give us no positive evidence for such.

Hebrews 6:2 is another descriptive statement that includes reference to the Christian water rite. It tells us that water baptism has to do with the elementary doctrine or instructions of the Christian faith, with the beginnings of Christian life. This verse also tells us that the rite was normally associated with repentance, faith, and the laying on of hands and basic doctrine. Thus, at least in this Jewish Christian community, water baptism was probably a rite only for those who could exercise repentance, express faith, or receive elementary instruction. On further reflection, we must remember that those statements in Acts were not merely descriptive in nature, for Luke selected them out of a host of possible events to illustrate his points about missions, the work of the Spirit, and so forth. It is not likely that he ever chose these texts with the intention of teaching his audience about water baptism, but incidentally, he does teach us that Luke saw water baptism as normally associated with repentance, faith, or a call to either of these, or a willingness to be baptized, or a desire to prepare for Spirit Baptism.

There are two probable explanations for this phenomenon. First, Luke is talking about Jewish Christians, as is the author of Hebrews, and they had long since been given a covenant sign. But second, in both Hebrews and Acts this way of talking about water baptism and associating it with things like repentance is partly due to the fact that these authors lived in an age when the church was primarily missionary, and thus in Luke's time, second-generation problems were only beginning to arise.

One may argue, however, that by A.D. 70 or 80 someone must have asked what was to be done with children of Christian parents. Surely Luke was at least beginning to take such problems into consideration. This argument is not without force, and inasmuch as Luke-Acts was written to serve the church of Luke's day, then his assertion of the normalcy of adult baptism and his silence on infant baptism may be more important than a Paedo-Baptist would be normally comfortable admitting. The same goes with Paul, though to a lesser degree, and also with the Fourth Evangelist, who never mentions the water rite other than possible allusions to Jesus' experience at the Jordan. In addition, 1 Peter 3:21, if it sees water baptism as a sign of a pledge of someone to go on and live a Christian life and as something other than circumcision, probably also sees water baptism as normally an adult rite. It is one thing to dedicate one's child to God, but can one pledge that he or she will go on to live a Christian life? That seems to be a pledge of faith that only the baptized should or could make. As we have said, however, *appeal* rather than *pledge* may be the better word to use in translating 1 Peter 3:21, and if this is correct certainly the water baptism of an infant can be an appeal to God that this child will go on and live a Christian life "in good conscience."

THE BOUNDARY MARKER

Water baptism is an act of the community in the process of making disciples (Matt 28:19-20). It is an act of "signing" someone who is, or normally ought to be, between Golgotha and his own personal Pentecost. In this, water baptism is a sign of the promise of the Spirit yet to come. It may be argued that since the promise is to "you and your children" (Acts 2:39), then our children should also receive the sign of the promise. This cannot be ruled out. If Jeremias is right about the reading of Acts 2:39 ("to us and our children") or even if he is right about Justin Martyr's belief in infant baptism, which I think he is, then we have clear evidence that the church as early as A.D. 150 thought that infant baptism was an acceptable practice.[3]

I have tried to show in this study that there was a good presacramental basis and train of thought in the New Testament that could make such a practice meaningful, though not as meaningful for the baptized person as adult baptism itself. Kurt Aland, after arguing that infant baptism cannot be found in the New Testament or in history until the third century, was willing to accept infant baptism as a legitimate deduction from New Testament theology. He agrees with Oscar Cullmann that the New Testament is not only silent about infant baptism, but also about the baptism of Christian children as adults. We must quote Aland's remarks at length because they are helpful and important:

(1) The New Testament undoubtedly makes statements about the character and significance of baptism for the Christian, but it makes these statements without providing any binding

prescription as to the manner in which it is to be carried out, and in particular without any clearly binding directions concerning the time of its administration.

(2) Here the [later] argument of Cyprian is still valid: "The mercy and grace of God is not to be refused to any human being." For the practice of infant baptism today can claim that it fulfills in a new time and in a new way what took place in early times in a different manner.

(3) Allow me to cite some of his [Luther's] words: "In the third place, as I have observed, they take their stand on this saying: 'He who believes and is baptized shall be saved.' They wish to infer from this that no one should be baptized until he believes. On the contrary I say that they venture upon great presumptuousness. For if they intend to follow out this notion they must not baptize until they know of a surety that the candidate for baptism does believe. But how and when can they ever know that? Have they become gods, so that they can see into the heart of the people and know whether they believe or not?" "You say, 'He confesses that he has faith,' etc. No, rather, keep confession out of it. The text does not say, 'He who confesses,' but 'He who believes.' His confession you have, certainly, but his faith you do not know; hence on your view you cannot satisfy this saying unless you also know his faith, because all men are liars and only God knows the heart. Whoever therefore will base baptism on the faith of the person seeking baptism must never baptize anyone, for even if you were to baptize a person a hundred times a day you cannot once know whether he believes." "It is true that a person should believe for baptism, but baptism should not be administered on the basis of faith. It is one thing to have faith and another to trust in faith and so be baptized on the grounds of faith. He who gets baptized on the basis of faith is not only uncertain, but is also an idolatrous denier of Christ; for he trusts and builds on something of his own, namely on a gift that God has given him,

and not on God's word alone, precisely as another builds and reposes trust on his strength, his riches, power, wisdom, holiness, which are also gifts given by God."[4]

In view of (3) above, Aland goes on to say:

(4) The baptism of a child at a later age, on the ground that now, of his own decision, he fulfils the presupposition of Mark 16:16 . . . carries with it the danger of perverting baptism. Faith is made a presupposition for baptism which a [person] brings with him—it is made into a work that he does.

(5) I do not get baptized, explains Luther, because I am sure of faith, but because God has commanded it and will have it. "For even though I were never more sure of faith, yet am I sure of the command, since God enjoins baptism, sending forth the command for the whole world, Here I can make no mistake, for God's command cannot deceive; but he has never said or demanded or ordered anything about my faith."[5]

These statements carry sound advice to which all must listen. Perhaps the best way to conclude this section is with an analogy first suggested by one of my colleagues. Water baptism is like enrollment in school, the school of Christ. Just as parents, apart from and without the consent of their offspring, enroll their children in school, so is the case of infant baptism. In neither case is it presumed that the child being enrolled/baptized already knows and accepts what is going to be taught.

On the other hand, when an adult enrolls in school, the situation changes. It is assumed that the adult enrolled under his own volition, has some knowledge of the content of the course, and has accepted the responsibilities of the course requirements. This is analogous to adult baptism since it is assumed that the adult has freely chosen baptism, has planned to or has already accepted Christ, and has expressed a desire to lead a Christian life. The new convert, like the student, has only the most rudimentary knowledge of the Christian life, the course content, but it is enough for him to make an informed choice and to commit himself to a life of learning and growing in the faith. Thus, baptism, like enrollment, is a pointe departe.

Water baptism then is not a confirmation that the pilgrimage is completed or even well under way, but it can be seen as a recognition that the journey has begun. It is a commitment in a certain direction, and it is also a recognition that God has already begun his work in the one being baptized. As Geoffrey Bromiley says: "If baptism tells us what we ourselves are to do, it bases this imperative on the indicative of what God has done, does, and will do for us. Hence baptism does not arise out of any work of ours. It is baptism into the work of God on our behalf."[6] The church will do well to recognize baptism for what it is—not a graduation exercise, but the first step in the process of the Christian life, enrollment in the school of Christ. As such, different Christians will view differently who can and may be enrolled in that school. In my view the analogies between circumcision and baptism in the New Testament, and the clear indications that baptism symbolizes the regenerative work of God and not our response to that work, decides the issue for me. I believe infants of believers should be enrolled in the school of Christ. If they are already a part of the new covenant community, albeit provisionally—if as Paul says they are "set apart" and Jesus said to such as these belongs his kingdom—why then should we refuse them the sign of the new covenant, an inclusive sign that both men and women alike can bear? I can think of no good reason.

Chapter 8

POSTSCRIPT

Coming Up for Air: Where Do We Go from Here?

At the start of my survey of the New Testament evidence I admitted to having doubts about infant baptism as a New Testament practice. Those doubts have been confirmed. Even the household texts of Acts rebound on the Paedo-Baptist's head under close scrutiny. I also argued that both traditional Baptist and Paedo-Baptist camps, and now I add the Occasionalists like Dunn or Beasley-Murray, have shipped some water and are in need of reform in regard to the practice of water baptism.

While Baptists have seen a connection of repentance, faith, and water baptism as normal in the New Testament, they have placed the order of baptisms, Spirit then water, in an abnormal or at least unusual arrangement. While Paedo-Baptists have gotten the order of water then Spirit correct, the order that is more often manifested in the New Testament, they have not paid proper attention to the fact that it was the normal practice in New Testament times to make a close connection between repentance, faith, and water baptism (cf. Heb 6). If I have not alienated my whole audience by this point, then perhaps they will hear me out as I make the following remarks and final suggestions.

First, it is wrong to assume without evidence that the proper recipients of Old Testament circumcision are the same as the proper recipients of New Testament water baptism. It is also wrong to assume without evidence that the necessary prerequisites for the baptism of an adult convert without prior association with Christ's body are the same as those for the baptism of an infant who is holy, having been granted a special, even if provisional, status by God. Since the New Testament does not tell us explicitly when the children of believing parents should be baptized, both Baptists and Paedo-Baptists are arguing from inference, not clear evidence.

It is a debatable question whose assumptions are justified about the children of believers on the basis of the New Testament evidence. Part of the debate that has not been settled is whether baptism is to be seen as an appeal for or a pledge to a Christian life. In its symbolism, baptism depicts not the work of humans, but of God. It is natural to assume that baptism presupposes the work of God in someone's life, so that the recipient's life in some way reflects what this sign symbolizes. It is, however, an open question whether or not God's work, whereby God declares the child of a believer holy, is sufficient to warrant baptizing that child. Clearly, the setting apart involved in a child's holiness, and the work of the Spirit involved in regeneration may not be the same thing, nor are they mutually exclusive. It could be argued that since baptism depicts regeneration, one should not baptize a child who may not be regenerated. On the other hand, there are serious difficulties with a covenantal theology that is led to the point of saying that infants of believers have no place among Abraham's seed and the new covenant community since they are incapable of faith and repentance.[1]

This is the logical conclusion of most, if not all, Baptist theology, and it is hard to see how such a theology can avoid admitting that even the infants of believers are lost until they have faith, since, on their own insistence, faith is the necessary prerequisite of baptism, entrance into the new covenant community, salvation, and so on. Interestingly, in practice, if not in principle, many Baptists recoil from treating their own children as "little pagans" or in the same position as the children of non-Christians. Texts such as 1 Corinthians 7:14, Acts 2:38-39, and Mark 10:14 and its parallels, rightly should give one pause before one is willing to assert that the children of believers are like the children of unbelievers: children of wrath, not children of grace, until they prove otherwise. That Paedo-Baptists believe that children of believers have a provisional place among God's people should not be thought to be a result of naive optimism, or some non-Christian notion about the sinlessness or guiltlessness of all children. This belief in the provisional place in the covenant is based not on sentiment, but on belief that the New Testament grants "such as these" a place within the kingdom with the numbers of the holy ones. It is well to add that there is a difference between innocence that is the opposite of experience, and blamelessness that is the opposite of sin. Infants by definition are not guilty of a willful violation of a known law, and hence a transgression. In that sense they can be said to be blameless before the commandments of God, and indeed innocent in the sense that sin is no part of their volitional behavior as of yet. This, however, does not settle the matter. If the Psalmist was right that all are conceived in sin—which is to say, if there is such a thing as an inherited fallen nature that comes to us from conception—then infants, even of believers, are not without the need of redemption. They are not naturally born in a state of grace, but there is a sanctifying influence of a Christian parent on such an infant, and 1 Corinthians 7 attests to this fact—this acquired state of holiness that does not come by personal choice or decision of faith.

The baptism of such an infant or small child recognizes that God's work has already begun in their lives before they could respond, and that since salvation is a process that goes on throughout one's life and is only completed and settled really at death and then more positively in the resurrection at Christ's return, it could never be a matter of waiting until a person is truly or fully saved to baptize them. We would be waiting until the eschaton in that case, or would be trapped in the early church dilemma where the church read Hebrews 6 to suggest that there could be no post-baptismal sins, and thus people from the highest to the lowest in the Kingdom (including Emperors like Constantine) were postponing their baptism until they were near death. This would be a complete violation of the nature of baptism which is a rite of passage, an initiatory rite marking when God has begun with you in your life, when God has begun to save you.

Second, infant baptism, while not a New Testament practice, cannot be ruled out as a legitimate theological development using the New Testament as a presacramental foundation. It is an honest attempt to deal with problems that only arose in force after the New Testament was written. This last fact makes Beasley-Murray's and Dunn's arguments suspect when they try to argue from the part (a missionary church beginning to work out its theology in New Testament times) to the whole. I believe that Scripture is inspired and is our canon and infallible rule for theology. This, however, does not rule out attempts to adopt and adapt New Testament practice and teaching to later and different situations, or to try and deduce what Paul or Peter or Luke would have said on the basis of what they did say. The descriptive and theological statements about water baptism and even the imperative statements such as Matthew 28:19-20 and Acts 2:38 are not of such a nature that infant baptism can be ruled out. Accordingly, I see no warrant for Barth's caustic remark that infant baptism is the "wound in the church." Nor do I see any justification for Beasley-Murray's conclusion that infant baptism is not Christian baptism and those experiencing it should be later rebaptized if they are willing. Even Barth, despite his own strong feelings, was not willing to go that far.

Third, because of the fact that water baptism then Spirit Baptism seems to have been the usual procedure in the New Testament, I think we should do likewise. The traditional Baptist order of Spirit Baptism then water baptism, or at least saving faith (reflecting the Spirit) then water baptism, is to be seen as abnormal and certainly not normative for the church today. With New Testament practice as our guide, it appears that as soon as a person gives evidence of belief or willingness to be baptized, we should baptize him. Acts 8 shows us that even some belief is no guarantee of saving faith, nor is a good confession for that matter. We must do our best to baptize with water those who are beginning to live a Christian life, for water baptism is meant to be preparatory for Spirit Baptism, not a confirmation of its prior reception. In all this, we must simply obey God—trying to make disciples by baptizing and teaching. The results are in God's hands. Only God can read an adult's or child's heart. If a person already has the Spirit, which will presumably manifest itself either in the Spirit's gifts or fruit, that person should receive water baptism as soon as possible, whatever their age. Water baptism should not be seen as the climax of a confirmation process, but as the beginning of an initiation process.

Fourth, all Christians should recognize, no matter which side of the baptismal waters they stand on, that Christian children are not in the same position as children of two pagan parents. First Corinthians 7:14 and Mark 10:14 and its parallels make this clear. Accordingly, there should be some required recognition of this fact from the beginning of their lives in a Christian family. For Baptists who are unwilling to baptize children, there could be a dedication rite. It helps neither the parents nor the children if the children are treated as proselytes; the children are holy, and the promise is said to be for them. All steps should be taken from birth to ensure that at some point they accept that promise. I think this should include an act by the community giving the children a special place in the midst of the church—an act of dedication and blessing as in Matthew 14:13, Luke 18:15, and Mark 10:16. As Luke 18:15 shows, this rite is for infants.

The advocates of occasionalism, while making valid points about some or most proselyte baptisms, must learn to take into account the fact that children of Christian parents often receive the Spirit in a quiet and lengthy process. Thus, they may receive water baptism long before, but hopefully not long after, they are willing to accept baptism and the Name it names. In either case, an insistence on a close-knit water baptism then Spirit Baptism as virtually one experience is a failure to recognize a Christian child's often lengthy initiation-conversion process. If insisted on for Christian children, this pattern will lead to their feeling inferior or in doubt of their faith if they do not have a dramatic Spirit Baptism or conversion experience.

But God nowhere promises us a dramatic Damascus road experience. Normally that is only the experience of either those who enter the community of faith having been entirely outside that community in the past, or it is the experience of those who wander away from the community in a drastic fashion and then suddenly are convicted and convinced to repent at some juncture. Bromiley rightly says, "The children of confessing Christians awaken to self-conscious life with the promise of the gospel in their ears and may thus have the mark of the covenant on their bodies. . . . The call to them is not to enter into a totally new covenant relationship proclaimed for the first time from outside."[2]

Fifth, to this point I have said things that the Baptist, more than the Paedo-Baptist, needs to hear. Now I reverse the procedure. In the first place, water baptism is not necessary for salvation, as 1 Corinthians 1 makes clear. Repentance, belief, Spirit Baptism, Christian life, perseverance till death—these are necessary for salvation. Water baptism, however, is necessary if one wishes to obey our Lord's commands, and it is possible to obey the command in Matthew 28:19 in particular.

Sixth, water baptism is not an act of God, though it is a gift of God to the Christian community. It is an act of the community for someone who is beginning to be a Christian or is holy or set apart for God. Water baptism can be used as a visible sign of one's repentance and commitment to God, as a confession of faith, and as an appeal for the Spirit, but it is none of these things in itself. It is not Spirit Baptism, nor does it initiate one into Christ's body, nor does it necessarily convey grace. Acts 8:12ff. and the case of Simon Magus make this plain. Nothing should be ascribed to water baptism that only properly can be ascribed to Spirit Baptism. Only the latter is the seal of the new covenant. We are in the age of fulfillment, not just the age of promise where sign and seal were one since the promise itself was future. Water baptism is the sign of the covenant, not the seal of its reception.

Seventh, later baptism, however, must not be trivialized so it is thought to be merely a sort of circumcision or dedication rite. This is as bad as seeing it as a confirmation rite. Thus, water baptism must be preached for what it really is: a sign and powerful symbol of divine redemptive-judgment, of burial with Christ, of cleansing through the Spirit, of future Spirit Baptism, of the death of Christ, of the circumcision of our old nature, and possibly as an appeal for a Christian life. We should emphasize the idea of water baptism standing between Christ's death as a baptism, and our death to sin in Spirit Baptism. It symbolizes both. Baptism also symbolizes an ongoing work of God, which in fact is not completed until or after death when we are purged of all sin—dead to sin once and for all. Accordingly, it is wrong to teach or intimate that what water baptism symbolizes is some punctiliar work of God (conversion) or a singular decision or confession made by a human being. Salvation is something about which one must say, "I have been saved, I am being saved, and I shall be saved" if we are to be true to all that the New Testament says about soteriology.

Eighth, because infant baptism was not the normal sort of baptism the New Testament writers had in mind, I suggest that we should not treat it as the normal practice, much less the normative practice, of the modern church. This problem has several remedies. One is to emphasize missionary work and the baptism of adults even in Paedo-Baptist communities. Infant baptism of everyone substitutes a subsidiary practice for the primary practice of New Testament times. Water baptism was given originally as a tool of missionary work (Matt 28:19) and this emphasis must not be lost. A second remedy would be to emphasize the idea of infant dedication. Since water baptism is not necessary for salvation, ministers could suggest to parents to wait and have their children baptized when they themselves request it. Parents who feel strongly about going ahead with infant baptism should be allowed to do so, however. By allowing both options, perhaps even Paedo-Baptists can come closer to the normal practice of New Testament times without giving up their legitimate theological deductions.

Ninth, if the suggestions in point 8 are followed, then perhaps Paedo-Baptist churches will begin to appreciate water baptism for the rich symbol and sign that it is, rather than treating water baptism as simply a dedicatory rite. There is no doubt, however, that water baptism is more meaningful and more appropriate for those who receive it if they are of an age when they can at least begin to appreciate its significance. If 1 Peter 3:21 means "pledge," then those who are of an age who can pledge to go on to live a Christian life will be more nearly conforming to what baptism means in the New Testament. God's grace does go before us, but water baptism is not an act of grace. It is a result of the gracious acts involved in Jesus' death, resurrection, and Spirit giving. Water baptism is, however, a sign of the promise and, as such, Acts 2:39 reveals that it cannot be inappropriate to baptize even infants of Christian parents to whom the promise is also given.

Tenth, due attention must be given to baptismal discipline in all churches. Baptism is not for pagans, whether parents or children. Parents who wish for their children to be baptized should be carefully questioned as to their reasons, unless the minister already knows them to be followers of Jesus Christ. Undoubtedly, this places an extra responsibility on the minister, but the "sacraments" must not be profaned, for they both represent the death of Our Lord and his greatest gift for this age, the Spirit. These are gifts given exclusively to the church, as we see in Matthew 28:19, and must not be partaken of in an "unworthy manner" (1 Cor 11:27). Baptism and the Lord's Supper are not the loving handshake we offer to non-Christians visiting our church. There are preconditions for both. The Lord's Supper is the right hand of fellowship given to those who bear the name Christian or who at that very moment are prepared to truly and earnestly repent and receive the forgiving and healing grace of God. Baptism is for those who are crossing the boundary into the community and therefore may appropriately receive the rite of passage or initiation. May the Lord give us discernment in all these matters. In conclusion I leave the reader with a brief poem:

WATER RITES

Can sin be drowned in water,
E'en with a flood of tears?
Or is it rather Spirit
That grafts the sinner in?

Does parting of the waters
Make Exodus come true?
Or is it rather death to sin
The makes one born anew?

Between the two creations
Two baptisms confess
The one depicts the story,
The other makes one blest.

Immersion in Christ's story
Death, burial, new birth
Begins the tale of Christians,
New beings on old earth.

NOTES

Chapter 1

1   Karl Barth, *Church Dogmatics*, vol. 4 part 4 (trans. B. W. Bromiley; Edinburgh: T&T Clark, 1969), 47.

2   *Didache* 7.1-4. The translation is mine. You can find a new translation of this important early Christian work in Bart D. Ehrman, *The Apostolic Fathers*, vol. 1 (Cambridge: Harvard University Press, 2003), 405–43, here 429.

3   Karl Barth, *The Teaching of the Church Regarding Baptism* (trans. E. A. Payne; London: SCM Press, 1948), 43–44. P. K. Jewett (*Infant Baptism and the Covenant of Grace* [Grand Rapids: Eerdmans, 1978], 86) admits the ethico-theological implications of circumcision, but probably is wrong in seeing it as a symbol of the positive side of renewal. Further, he wrongly assumes that receiving the covenant sign was purely a matter of heredity in the Old Testament. Rather, it was a matter of association with the covenant and covenant keepers, and not always a matter of heredity. For example, bought slaves are included and could receive the covenant sign.

4   G. R. Beasley-Murray, *Baptism in the New Testament* (Grand Rapids: Eerdmans, 1962), 341.

5   P. Marcel, *The Biblical Doctrine of Infant Baptism* (trans. P. E. Hughes; London: J. Clark, 1953), 86.

6   O. Cullmann, *Baptism in the New Testament* (trans. J. K. S. Reid; London: SCM Press, 1950), 58.

7   Gerhard Von Rad, *Genesis* (Philadelphia: Westminster, 1972), 201.

8   J. B. Pritchard, ed. *Ancient Near Eastern Texts* (3d ed.; Princeton: Princeton University Press, 1969), 199ff.; B. S. Childs, *Exodus* (Philadelphia: Westminster, 1974), 348.

9   Meredith Kline, "Genesis," in *The New Bible Commentary Revised* (3d ed.; ed. D. Guthrie and J. A. Motyer; Grand Rapids: Eerdmans, 1970), 96–97.

10   Von Rad, 201.

11   Von Rad, 201.

12   H. Blair, "Joshua," in Guthrie and Motyer, *New Bible Commentary Revised*, 238.

13   C. F. Keil and F. Delitzsch, *Commentary on the Old Testament* (10 vols.; Grand Rapids: Eerdmans, 1975), 2:59.

14   Beasley-Murray, 338–40.

15   Childs, 308.

16   Beasley-Murray, 5.

17   Beasley-Murray, 6–7.

18   Beasley-Murray, 8.

19   The physical order is viewed as so closely connected to the spiritual that the language of the physical can be used to describe the spiritual.

20   See, e.g., J. Jeremias, *Infant Baptism in the First Four Centuries* (trans. D. Cairns; London: SCM Press, 1960), 24–25. More recent evidence has not really changed this judgment.

21   Beasley-Murray, 18–19. Most scholars agree that the *Testament of Levi* probably predates the turn of the era, and it does indeed refer to proselyte baptism.

22 G. F. Moore, *Judaism in the First Centuries of the Christian Era* (New York: Schocken Press, 1971), 332, and 109n101.

23 Moore, 332.

24 See Jeremias, *Infant Baptism*, 28 and n. 5. This dispute certainly went on prior to New Testament times. Jeremias believes the Hillelites won the day on this issue and that the impurity of a corpse was ascribed to Gentiles. See John 18:28; Matt 8:9; Josephus, *Ant.* 18.4.3.

25 Jeremias, *Infant Baptism*, 32–33.

26 Jeremias, *Infant Baptism*, 34–36.

27 Beasley-Murray, 24–25, 31–32.

28 See David Daube, *The New Testament and Rabbinic Judaism* (London: Athlone Press, 1956), 106–40; and Jeremias, *Infant Baptism*, 34–36.

29 Jeremias, *Infant Baptism*, 37–39.

30 Josephus, *War* 2.8.5-13. This conclusion is based on the assumption, now very widely accepted, that the Essenes were part of the Qumran community.

31 Beasley-Murray, 11.

32 Geza Vermes, *The Dead Sea Scrolls* (Harmondsworth: Penguin, 1965), 45.

33 Vermes, 45.

34 Beasley-Murray, 14.

Chapter 2

1 Beasley-Murray, 18.

2 See my lengthy discussion on John in my *The Christology of Jesus* (Minneapolis: Fortress, 1990).

3 J. A. T. Robinson, "The Baptism of John and the Qumran Community," in *Twelve New Testament Studies* (London: SCM Press, 1962), 11–27, here 12.

4 Robinson, 15.

5   Theodore H. Gaster, *The Dead Sea Scriptures* (Garden City, N.Y.: Doubleday, 1976), 53.

6   Robinson, 20.

7   James Dunn, *Baptism in the Spirit* (London: SCM Press, 1970), 9–10.

8   The verb ἐγγίζω means "to approach, to draw near."

9   Dunn, 15.

10 On the meaning of ἐίς μετάνοιάν ἡμάρτιαν, see Dunn, 14–16.

11 Dunn, 18.

12 Dunn, 14.

13 Beasley-Murray, 22.

14 Barth, *Church Dogmatic*, vol. 4 part 4, p. 62.

15 Barth, *Church Dogmatic*, vol. 4 part 4, p. 67.

16 Barth, *Church Dogmatic*, vol. 4 part 4, p. 58.

17 See Dunn, 20–21; C. K. Barrett, *The Gospel according to St. John* (London: SPCK, 1955), 182.

18 See my discussion in Witherington, *The Gospel of Matthew* (Macon, Ga.: Smythe & Helwys, 2006), ad loc.

19 Beasley-Murray, 49.

20 Beasley-Murray, 51.

21 I am assuming for the sake of argument that John actually said this. Of course many commentators disagree, but see my *John's Wisdom* (Louisville, Ky.: Westminster John Knox, 1995), ad loc. If John did not say this, or something close to it, then this point is moot.

22 Dunn, 26.

23 Dunn, 26. See my *The Gospel of Mark* (Grand Rapids: Eerdmans, 2000), ad loc.

24 Dunn, 27.

25 Dunn, 28.

26 Dunn, 33n34.

27 This may not have been plain to him until later, closer to the time when he spoke such sayings as Mark 10:38. The imagery of judg-

ment depicted in baptismal immersion may have conjured up the idea of death in Jesus' mind as he underwent the rite. Certainly, baptism can be seen as a figure of divine wrath or at least impending disaster. As Dunn remarks, "In the Old Testament the river and the flood are used as metaphors for being overwhelmed by calamities (Ps. 42.7; 69.2,15; Isa. 32.2)" (11). This notion probably stands behind Mark 10:38 and Luke 12:50.

28 The αὐτοῖς in Matthew 19:13 is significant, for it indicates that it was not just mothers bringing their children, but must have also involved fathers or older children bringing them as well.

29 The word Luke uses is βρέφος. In one other place in Luke-Acts it clearly means infants—even a prenatal infant—not just a small child (cf. Luke 1:41, 44; 2:12, 16; Acts 7:12. The normal meaning of the word is indeed "infant" or "small child."

30 Jeremias, *Infant Baptism*, 49–50.

31 The verb here carries the sense of being absolutely indignant, quite angry.

32 Beasley-Murray, 327.

33 Cullmann, 71–80.

34 Cullmann, 75.

35 Cullmann, 78.

36 Jeremias, *Infant Baptism*, 51–55.

37 F. A. Schilling, "What Means the Saying about Receiving the Kingdom of God as a Little Child–Mk. X.15, Lk.xviii.17," *Expository Times* 77 (1965): 58.

38 Schilling, 56–58.

39 Beasley-Murray, 324–25.

40 Beasley-Murray, 324n4.

41 Jewett, 123–36.

42 Jeremias, *Infant Baptism*, 44–48; and G. W. Bromiley, *Children of Promise–The Case for Baptizing Infants* (Grand Rapids: Eerdmans, 1979), 8–9.

43 Jeremias, *Infant Baptism*, 46–48.

44　One could argue that even if one sees the new covenant as largely distinct from the old covenant, still the principles in regard to the covenantal sign could be analogous. In my view it is not so much a matter of the new covenant continuing or renewing the old, as that some aspects of the old covenant be reaffirmed in the new. The question then is whether the rite-of-passage ritual in some respects is one of these things.

45　Beasley-Murray, 194.

46　Beasley-Murray, 195–96.

47　Beasley-Murray, 195.

48　Beasley-Murray, 198.

49　J. Jeremias, *The Origins of Infant Baptism* (trans. D. M. Baron; London: SCM Press, 1963), 80–81.

50　Beasley-Murray, 198.

Chapter 3

1　Dunn, 42.

2　Dunn, 44–54.

3　Dunn, 47–48.

4　Beasley- Murray, 342–43.

5　B. M. Metzger, *A Textual Commentary on the Greek New Testament* (London: United Bible Societies, 1971), 296–97.

6　Jeremias, *Infant Baptism*, 72.

7　Jeremias, *Origins*, 12–32.

8　E. Stauffer, "Zur Kindertaufe in der Urkirche," *Deutsches Pfarrerblatt* 49 (1949): 152–54.

9　Jeremias, *Origins*, 12–32.

10　Jeremias, *Origins*, 13.

11　Jeremias, *Origins*, 19–21.

12　Dunn, 79–82.

13　See J. Bowman, "Samaritan Studies," *BJRL* 40 (1957–1958): 298–327.

14　See Dunn, 55–72.

15 λόγος here could just mean matter or ministry even, but whatever
its denotation, it connotes that Simon is refused a share or "lot" in
Christian ministry, and probably even in Christianity itself. The
phrase "you shall have no lot/share" comes from the LXX and
can be seen as a form of excommunication. See Deut 12:12 and
14:27.

16 See Acts 24:14 and 26:27; cf. Dunn, 65.

17 As far as we can tell, while immersion would seem to best comport
with what baptism was seen to symbolize in the early church, the
mode of baptism seems to have depended on the quantity and sort
of water readily available in a "dry and weary land." Christians
could not very well baptize their converts in Jewish mikvehs, and
the Jordan and the ocean were not near to everyone that was converted. The text we cited at the beginning of this study comes out
of early Jewish Christianity and reflects these logistical problems,
which too few take into account these days. In any case, what we
see in Acts are missionary baptisms, which do not tell us how the
rite would be practiced once there were second- and third-genera-
tion Christians with infants.

18 Metzger, 360. The earliest evidence from the church Fathers is
from Irenaeus at the end of the second century.

19 J. A. T. Robinson, "Elijah, John, and Jesus," in *Twelve New Testament Studies*, 28–52 esp. 49.

20 Kirsopp Lake, *The Beginnings of Christianity*, 6 vols. (ed. J. Foakes-
Jackson; London: Macmillan 1920–1933), 5:231

21 Beasley-Murray, 112; cf. Dunn, 189.

22 Dunn, 84–85.

23 Dunn, 86–89.

24 Dunn, 74.

25 See Dunn, 76–77 and John 9:39-41; Acts 26:18; 2 Cor 4:4-6; Heb
6:4, 10:32.

26 Dunn, 80.

27 Dunn, 76.

Chapter 4

1 See Beasley-Murray, 112.
2 On this whole discussion it is most helpful to read through M. G. Kline's article "Oath and Ordeal I" which was in *WTJ* (1965) and now is available online at http://www.apuritansmind.com/ Baptism/KlineMeredithOathOrdealPart1.html.
3 Douglas Moo, *The Epistle to the Romans* (Grand Rapids: Eerdmans, 1996), 366.
4 See my discussion in *Paul's Letter to the Romans: A Socio-Rhetorical Commentary* (Grand Rapids: Eerdmans, 2004), 155–59.
5 Dunn, 185–86.
6 W. A. Meeks, *The First Urban Christians* (New Haven: Yale University Press, 2003), 150.
7 Meeks, 153.
8 Beasley-Murray, 113.
9 See Dunn, 185.

Chapter 5

1 Dunn, 186.
2 Dunn, 190.
3 See my *John's Wisdom*, ad loc.
4 For a detailed version of this argument, see Ben Witherington III, "The Waters of Birth: John 3.5 and 1 John 5.6-8," *New Testament Studies* 35 (1989): 155–60.
5 Beasley-Murray, 216–32. I pass over here such texts as John 5, 7:38, 9:7, 13, which Beasley-Murray has very adequately dealt with. He has shown that at most we have sacramental language used in these texts, without any discussion of sacraments.
6 Beasley-Murray, 225.
7 I pass over 1 John 2:20, 27 and 3:9 which do not likely refer to anything other than the anointing by, of, and through God's Spirit. See Dunn, 195–200 and Ben Witherington III, *Letters and the*

Homilies of the New Testament, 3 vols. (Downers Grove, Ill.: Inter-
Varsity, 2006), vol. 1, ad loc.

8   In my view the author of 1 John is the source of the material in the
fourth gospel, but not the final editor of that gospel.

9   Dunn, 200–202; Beasley-Murray, 263–65.

10   Dunn, 202.

Chapter 6

1   See Witherington, *Letters and Homilies,* vol. 2, on Hebrews.

2   Dunn, 206–7.

3   Dunn, 207–8; Beasley-Murray, 243–45.

4   Dunn, 213–14. Emphasis added by me.

5   See my *Letters and Homilies,* vol. 3.

6   Beasley-Murray, 254–60; cf. Dunn, 220–24.

7   Dunn, 216; and Beasley-Murray, 259.

8   Metzger, 643; Dunn, 216.

9   R. T. France, "Exegesis in Practice," in *New Testament Interpretation*
(ed. I. H. Marshall; Exeter: Pater Noster Press, 1977), 253–81, here
273–74.

10   Rightly Dunn, 217.

11   Cf. Jer 4:4; 1 Sam 17:26, 36; Jer 9:26; Philo, *Spec. Laws* 1.2–7; esp.
1.5.

12   See J. N. D. Kelly, *A Commentary on the Epistles of Peter and Jude*
(London: A&C Black, 1969), 161–62; France, 281n59.

13   E. G. Selwyn, *The First Epistle of Peter* (London: Macmillan, 1974),
205.

14   France, 274–75, lays out the evidence well.

15   C. Mauer, "συνείδησις," *TDNT* 7 (1971): 918–19. See France,
275.

Chapter 7

1   Dunn, 214.

2   Beasley-Murray, 340.

3 Jeremias, *Origins*, 26–27.
4 K. Aland, *Did the Early Church Baptize Infants?* (trans. G. R. Beasley-Murray; London: SCM Press, 1963), 114–15.
5 Aland, 115.
6 Bromiley, 107.

Postscript

1 Jewett, 170, 238–39.
2 Bromiley, 45.

INDEX